OTHER TITLES OF INTEREST FROM ST. LUCIE PRESS

Continual Improvement in Government: Tools and Methods

Teams in Government: A Handbook for Team-Based Organizations

Quality Government: Designing, Developing, and Implementing TQM

Improving Service Quality: Achieving High Performance in the Public and Private Sectors

Leadership by Encouragement

The Skills of Encouragement: Bringing Out the Best in Yourself and Others

Creating Productive Organizations

The Motivating Team Leader

Organization Teams: Building Continuous Quality Improvement

The New Leader: Bringing Creativity and Innovation to the Workplace

Quality Improvement Handbook: Team Guide to Tools and Techniques

For more information about these titles call, fax or write:

St. Lucie Press
100 E. Linton Blvd., Suite 403B
Delray Beach, FL 33483
TEL (407) 274-9906 • FAX (407) 274-9927

S$^t_{L}$

TRANSFORMATIONAL LEADERSHIP in GOVERNMENT

Jerry W. KOEHLER

Joseph M. PANKOWSKI

S^{t}_{L}

St. Lucie Press
Delray Beach, Florida

TABLE OF CONTENTS

PREFACE

Challenges for leaders have never been greater. The 1990s will be remembered for corporation mergers, downsizing, restructuring, and layoffs. The necessity for change, driven by the need to be competitive in a world economy, has been a subject for every daily newspaper, weekly magazine, and TV talk show.

The call for change is especially true for leaders in government, in view of the revolution of its citizens calling for fewer taxes, smaller budgets, less control, and more programs that actually work. Government is seen as a huge bureaucracy, entrenched in a false compassion for its citizens, measured not by outcomes, but rather by the dollars it consumes. Government is viewed as "the problem," rather than as a solution.

Clearly, there is a need for change in the way government is administered and managed that will regain the public's trust. Fortunately, there are fundamental methods and strategies that can accomplish these needed changes. They are "fundamental" in that the traditional bureaucracies, which stifle innovation and change, must be replaced by systems that encourage and empower every worker, from top to bottom, to create the smaller, more efficient and responsive government demanded by its owners—taxpayers.

One of the most difficult changes for American organizations during the past decade has been to shift from "top down" management systems to ones that empower the work force. Although many organizations have given lip service in the past to the importance of respecting the opinions of workers, American managers often found it very difficult to trust the wisdom of subordinates. Government administrators have found this transition to be even more difficult, in that external forces have not dramatically affected change. Whereas external forces made American businesses realize that if they were going to be competitive, they had to have fewer managers and workers, competition has played a smaller role in government, with "privatization" a minor threat at best.

Although government organizations are under severe attack by taxpayers and legislators, and are often forced to do more with less, empowering the government work force has not been totally embraced by government administrators. We believe that government administrators over time will be forced to change and will be expected to follow the organization models developed by some of our most competitive business organizations. Furthermore, enlightened government leaders have already accepted the premise that the key to government efficiency and effectiveness is an empowered government worker.

This book is written strictly for government leaders to describe how transformational leadership works in government. The idea for this book emerged when the authors were given the opportunity to implement Total Quality Management in the Department of Labor and Employment Security in Florida. One of the more difficult challenges in implementing TQM was to convince administrators to "rethink" their role in government. For years, administrators have been conditioned to believe that their job was to "do the thinking" and the job of their subordinates was to "do what they were told to do." Most administrators were only concerned with their "position power" and how to motivate people to behave the way they wanted them to behave. We wrote this book because few government administrators could easily grasp their new role after we asked them to empower their work force. Most of the time they would respond with, "What am I going to do now that you have taken all my power away from me?"

We, of course, were seeking leaders and not administrators. We were looking for people who were more concerned with improving government, not just managing people. We searched the literature for a book, or even an article, which was designed for government administrators on their role in empowering their work force. Having found none, we carefully noted and recorded the developing characteristics and behaviors of transformational leaders in our programs. This book is a result of those observations and analysis.

There are many people we need to thank for their assistance in publishing this book. First, we would like to thank the Governor of the state of Florida, Lawton Chiles, and the Lieutenant Governor, Buddy McKay, for giving us the opportunity to implement continual improvement teams in government. Second, we thank the internal consultants in the Department of Labor and Employment Security, the training staff, process improvement guides and all of our associates who are dedicated to improving Florida's government.

We owe a special thanks to Linda Plymale who typed the manuscript and to our publisher, Dennis Buda, our project supervisor, Sandra Pearlman, and production editor, Sandra Koskoff.

ABOUT THE AUTHORS

Dr. Jerry W. Koehler is a member of the faculty in the Department of Management at the University of South Florida in Tampa, currently serving as consultant to the office of the Governor, state of Florida. He served for three years as Deputy Secretary in the Florida Department of Labor and Employment Security.

Dr. Koehler has authored numerous books and has served as consultant to government agencies and leading business organizations. He is co-author with Joseph Pankowski of *Quality Government: Designing, Developing and Implementing TQM*, (St. Lucie Press, 1996), and two additional St. Lucie titles, *Teams in Government* and *Continual Improvement in Government: Tools and Methods*.

Joseph M. Pankowski is no stranger to quality improvement efforts, having directed the Bureau of Quality Assurance in the Florida Department of Labor and Security for five years prior to working with Dr. Koehler. He continues serving as a consultant to the Department on quality management, and conducts seminars on customer expectations, teams, tools, and presentation skills.

During his 31 years of work with government, he has experience as a first-line rehabilitation counselor, state supervisor and assistant director, in addition to other assignments. He has directed teams studying innovative approaches in service delivery, and under his guidance the Bureau of Quality Assurance was recognized by the federal government for its excellence.

CHAPTER 1

NEW DIRECTIONS IN LEADERSHIP

Give the worker a chance to work with pride.

—W. Edwards Deming, *Out of the Crisis*

We live in a time when change is swift and often abrupt. Technology changes so quickly that even people and organizations who have made it their business to change sometimes fall behind. Organizations and people who hesitate slightly can fall far behind in a short period of time. Not long ago, many administrators in leading American organizations believed that if they were cognizant of technological changes, and adapted these changes to their organization, they could be successful. History has told us, however, that it wasn't so easy. For example, automobile manufacturers in America led the world in technology advancements in building automobiles. Yet, at the same time, the American automobile manufacturers were losing many of their customers to foreign competitors. What we learned in industry was that even the most sophisticated technology was not the answer to maintaining success.

Like American industry, government leaders followed the same path. Leaders assumed that technology was the answer to government woes. It seemed as though every government organization was in a race to purchase the latest technology, and once this technology was installed, huge gains in productivity would be forthcoming.

Two significant problems emerged from the heavy reliance on technology to solve government problems. First, using technology to replace the old process frequently yielded ineffective results. Information systems consultants promised high returns for the money, and frequently delivered very little. Fortunately, a number of information systems consultants finally recognized that not allowing the "front-liners," the people who actually do the work, to help with the design and the development of systems was a primary reason the system changes failed to work effectively. Even experts with vast knowledge on specific subjects learned to recognize that they did not have all of the answers.

Leaders in government also learned a very costly lesson. They cannot delegate quality to outside consulting experts. For example, the former secretary of the umbrella health and rehabilitative services agency in Florida believed that if his organization was to improve the quality of its service, it was necessary to purchase an extremely expensive information system developed by a major company. This agency, the Department of Health and Rehabilitative Services (HRS), was one of the largest state agencies in the country, responsible for health programs, welfare payments, services for children, and other family services programs. One of the department's major problems was a payment error rate so high that it overpaid welfare recipients $100 million practically every year of its existence.

This decision proved to be very costly. While welfare workers were battling the day-to-day problems, the technology consultants were designing a system that was to be a cure-all for their problems. For some reason, leaders in HRS believed that a team of outsiders could do much better than a team of insiders.

Elected officials and political appointees are constantly in search of that one answer which will solve government's problem. Many political appointees and elected officials think the answers are outside of government, and that the brain power within government is too minimal to be useful. It is a sign of the times. Voters continually search for a miracle leader to save government, and once people get elected to office, they look for the miracle cure, which thus far in history has not been found.

Another problem emerged from the overemphasis on technology to solve government problems. Perhaps it is more serious. By overemphasizing technology, government leaders have alienated many government workers. Morale is often very low in government organizations, and workers have become disenfranchised from their organizations. It is not uncommon to hear once loyal and committed workers state that they "can't wait for their retirement." People who have never worked in a government organization cannot comprehend why government workers are so negative, when they have a "guaranteed job" and a reliable retirement program. Outsiders cannot understand government employees, who lament about being "beaten up for years" or complain about "being blamed for everything that goes wrong and never appreciated for doing a good job."

With the assumption that technology was the savior and government workers were a menace or a problem, administrators without leadership skills were frequently appointed throughout government. These administrators were people who were looking for answers, not with the people who worked for them, but rather with an outside source or with someone above them. Administrators were not offered appointments for their humanistic skills, but rather for their technical skills. When the authors were leading a major quality transformation in the Department of Labor and Employment Security in Florida, we were constantly amazed by the attitude of government administrators. Long-time veterans would continually suggest that they would be more effective and could get better results if they could only hire new people and had more money for technology. It was as though they never made the connection between their leadership skills and organizational results. It was as though they never saw themselves as the problem. They never seemed to comprehend the relationship between their own behavior and quality results.

For example, a very intelligent director of one of our divisions in the Department of Labor and Employment Security was a very astute, hard working administrator with superior technical skills, who never seemed to make a connection between her "hide in her office" behavior and quality results. As she searched in vain for technical solutions, her organization was falling apart at the bottom of the organization. She would write well-composed memorandums telling others how they ought to behave, such as "work in teams" and "cooperate with each other," while she remained isolated from the troops.

This case was not an isolated incident. We found that many government administrators took the position that solutions to organizational problems could only be found within management and their selected "in group." While implementing a quality initiative within a department that had over 7,000 employees, we found that we were able to easily work around administrators and strongly influence many of their subordinates. We had a number of top administrators who rejected the concept that front-line involvement was necessary to improve government. However, while the elitist administrators were searching for solutions, we were able to establish credibility with the front-line associates. We used the term "associates," rather than employees, because we believe there should not be a major distinction between employees and managers. In an empowered organization, front-liners are not employees who take orders, but associates who are expected to behave like managers in improving their processes. In fact, in an empowered organization, one can think of everyone as managers. Their job is to work with others to manage processes. Associates look to leaders for direction and support, but look to themselves and their associates for ways to improve the organization.

There were so many top administrators who did not understand leadership that we were able to fill the leadership void by working with lower-level personnel who emerged as "true" leaders. This led us to a conclusion that the most significant problem in the government today is the lack of leadership within government.

PURPOSE OF THIS BOOK

The purpose of this book is to redirect and re-energize leadership in government. We strongly believe that government administrators are committed to improving the quality of our government, but many have fallen into the trap that business administrators fell into during the 1970s and 1980s. The trap that caught business administrators was that leadership seemed to mean that leaders were supposed to provide solutions to problems. True leadership is not knowing the answers to technical problems, but rather providing a working environment that allows those closest to the problem to solve the problem.

We suggest that leadership in government needs to dramatically change its approach. We believe that the problem in government is that top management consistently searches for radical changes in its organization and is missing the point. We believe that radical change should occur in leaders, and that an environment could be established where government workers are able to focus on continual improvement, rather than radical improvements. This book describes what new government leaders need to know, need to do, and how to do it.

TRADITIONAL APPROACHES TO LEADERSHIP IN GOVERNMENT

Today's leadership in government frequently holds the following beliefs:

1. Leaders are administrators.

Many leaders see their job as one of administration. They interpret what the legislature or top management expects from them to administer the program according to legislation. Their job is provide order and direction with the quest for efficiency. Their focus is on structuring the organization so there is a division of labor and a hierarchy of authority.

2. Administrators are reactive.

Once the division of labor and hierarchy of authority are in place, the job of the administrator is to effectively react to problems that emerge in the bureaucracy. Government has been so entrenched with the traditional model of leadership that it is not unusual for individuals to be promoted into a leadership position because they have reacted well to a bureaucratic problem. For example, we have observed over the years that many government leaders earn accolades within government when they have reacted effectively and efficiently to a major problem. In one case, a leader was promoted into a very high position after dealing effectively with Hurricane Andrew. Another was promoted after effectively handling the press following the murder of an English visitor at a Florida rest stop. On a much smaller magnitude, we have observed people in government being promoted for solving problems that could have been easily solved with effective management systems. Traditionally, government has acknowledged the wisdom of people who have reacted well to legislators' and top government requests. It appears that one of the best ways to be promoted within government is to be in the right place at the right time and respond logically to a problem or a request.

3. Administrators direct activity.

Government plans and budgets are carefully laid out by legislative staffs and departments. The job of the leader is to carry out those plans within budget. Therefore, there should be unity of command and direction. All activities should be pointed toward the same objective. Top management interprets the legislation, defines the objectives, and passes these objectives down the organizational hierarchy. Administrators at each level receive orders from their superiors, and their job is to see that the objectives are met. The assumption is that if the objectives are correct and each person in the organization completes their part, their task, the objectives will be met.

4. Administrators maintain control.

Government administrators frequently assume that their job is to control the behavior of others. Since the typical attitude of a government administrator is that their job is to "pass it down," they have to find ways to control those below them so that what is passed down gets done. Therefore, to ensure that work gets done, rules and regulations are implemented to govern the organization.

Performance is then defined by employees as "getting what the administrator wants done" within the rules and regulations prescribed. A good leader is fair and uniformly applies rules to all employees.

5. Administrators cope with the status quo.

Government leaders frequently complain about the status quo, and on occasion, joke about the superficial knowledge legislators and appointed officials have about their programs. However, these same leaders perceive their job is not to change the status quo, but rather to endure it. Their attitude is that they can only do "the best they can" in their situation. To many government leaders, "initiative" means exerting energy to meet the quotas passed to them.

Several years ago, before the agency where we worked implemented a quality initiative focusing on customer service, one administrator was promoted because he was able to motivate the counselors in his office to "close" more cases (in this case, put people with disabilities back to work). He was able to achieve these phenomenal results because he emphasized the fact that the "state office" liked counselors who produced results. His emphasis on serving individuals with relatively minor disabilities resulted in more cases being closed successfully. All were legal closures; however, those persons with more severe disabilities may not have received the attention they needed to become successful. This administrator knew that top managers wanted to have a good record of case closures so that they could get more money from the federal government. Reaching this objective was easy, by not focusing on the severely disabled and instead, focusing on people with minor disabilities. He knew all along what he was doing. He was working within the framework established by the government. He accepted the status quo and learned how to use it to his advantage. Rather than trying to change government so that it would be more customer-oriented, it was to his advantage to maintain the status quo. Today that program no longer stresses closures, but instead stresses quality customer service, and individuals with severe disabilities are actually given priority.

There is another reason why government leaders may support the status quo. Often leaders feel they have "paid their dues" by working their way up the career ladder. They often have twenty or more years service with the agency and realize that any change in the status quo might jeopardize their position. There are already numerous threats to their existence from outsiders who are constantly looking at ways to "down size" or "right size" government. In addition, their very existence is threatened every four years should a new governor be elected. Furthermore, each new administration brings in "their" new leadership, through political appointments, to change government. Rarely does a department have the same politically appointed leader more than four years. For administrators to take an additional risk, by questioning the status quo, just adds to their uncertainty.

CHARTING A NEW LEADERSHIP PATH IN GOVERNMENT

The primary problem with government bureaucracies is that they are too rigid and too formal. Congress, state legislators, and appointed officials are constantly in search of a "new" bureaucracy. They believe that they can formulate the policies and hire administrators to impose them. However, as we approach the twenty-first century, it is time we realize that if government is to be effective, leadership in government must change. Elected and political officials cannot continue to believe that it is their job to "reinvent government" every four years, but rather to entrust and expect the leaders in government agencies to develop management systems that meet or exceed the expectations of the customers they serve.

To gain political support, taxpayer support, and customer support, government leaders are going to be asked to lead, not follow; to change the status quo, not accept it; to be proactive, not reactive; to control systems, not focus only on rules and regulations; to be leaders, not administrators; to be innovative, not complacent; to work in teams, rather than individually on tasks; and to initiate change, rather than criticize it.

One of the most significant problems we now have in government is that too many leaders have been selected and promoted because they embrace the traditional government administrator model. They have advanced because they have seen themselves as administrators, not leaders. They have advanced because they limited their risk and have accepted the status quo. They have advanced because they have reacted well to problems when they emerged. They have advanced because they have met the objectives sent from the top.

If government is going to survive and thrive in the twenty-first century, today's government leaders must dramatically change their approach to leadership. Taxpayers have lost confidence in government. Opinion polls show that less than 20 percent of the American public believe that government is efficient and effective. Unless government leaders change, traditional government practices will be encouraged and maintained. We believe the most effective action is to retrain government leaders with new principles of leadership so that government can embark upon a new way of conducting business.

During the past four years, the authors have been able to work with numerous leaders in state government when they initiated Total Quality Management in the Department of Labor and Employment Security in Florida. The first author served as the Deputy Secretary for the department, and the second author served as TQM Administrator. Although many top leaders rejected TQM and were unwilling to take the risk associated with changing an organization, others were willing. What was exciting was that once top administrators were willing to accept new principles of leadership, their subordinates caught the new wave and climbed aboard. This book describes the proven principles of leadership that directed our agency's new direction in quality—ones that will help others in changing the way their government programs serve customers.

DEFINING LEADERSHIP IN GOVERNMENT

Understanding leadership in government requires knowledge about bureaucracies. "Bureaucracy," to many people, has a negative connotation, and often implies an organizational structure that is swollen with uncaring employees and that is practically impossible to navigate. However, a bureaucracy can also be perceived as a structure that was carefully designed to administer government services. Leaders in government are often referred to as bureaucrats, a term with the connotation of being primarily interested in demonstrating power over customers. Rather than being seen as facilitators, leaders are often seen as obstacles. Government customers, when they do not get what they expect from an agency, are often highly critical and sometimes downright insulting. Government leaders often are abused, and for the most part, unappreciated by many of their customers. It is not uncommon for government leaders to isolate themselves from government customers, especially after years of abuse. Government leaders are constantly criticized by not only their customers, but also by their superiors and elected officials.

One of the primary problems with government is that leadership principles have largely been drawn from concepts that pertain to business organizations. Frequently, one hears business leaders extol the virtues of business and criticize government leaders for not running their organizations like a business. Many government leaders will agree with business leaders because they are frustrated with their attempts to change government. It is not uncommon to visit a government leader's office and find all of the recent books on leadership, written primarily for the business organization, on their bookshelves.

Many, but not all, of the management principles used in the private sector can be effectively implemented in government organizations. For example, the principles of Total Quality Management can definitely be applied to government organizations. However, to suggest that leadership principles which work at General Motors will also work in government is a fallacy. Bottom-line business organizations cause behaviors in leaders that are notably different from those found in government organization. Leadership styles and behaviors are significantly affected by organizational goals, situation, and culture. We often think of leadership in business organizations as a game. Effective leaders in business frequently are bent on encountering situations where they must win. Although business leaders like to think that they are developing a "win-win" situation, they know they do not want to lose.

Therefore, leadership can be defined in the business environment, as a process where the leader successfully influences the activities of others towards advancing the goals and growth of the business.

On the other hand, government organizations are not influenced by the bottom line, but rather by the results of legislation and customer service. Government leaders not only influence activities of others, but also must direct a course of action handed to them by legislation. Therefore, government leadership is defined as "**a process of influencing others and directing the course of action promulgated by legislation.**" This is not to suggest that the only option available to government leaders is to administer legislative programs. On the contrary, it suggests that leaders work within the boundaries of legislation applicable to their programs. However, within these confines, government leaders have many options. In fact, the goal of a government agency might well be to limit growth, such as welfare, food stamps, workers compensation, etc.

Not long ago Florida sponsored a seminar where representatives of major corporations lectured state government leaders on what they were doing to improve quality in their organizations. The reaction of most government leaders was, "that is nice, but it won't work here." Business leaders were very disappointed because government leaders were so close-minded to new ideas. In fact, we were irritated by the reception the representatives from business and industry were given by government leaders. However, it is possible to understand this cool reception when one acknowledges that government leaders and business leaders often do not speak the same language. People from business and industry are unfamiliar with government processes and the principles of government management. On the other hand, government leaders often do not understand how major corporations work and manage their businesses.

What is not so apparent is that leadership skills and expertise are not as easily transferable as most people believe. We have observed top business leaders take a job in government management and fail. We have seen exceptionally well-educated, ivy league professionals take a position in government and fail. We have observed generals come to work in state government, only to fail. The reverse is also true, for we have seen top government leaders take senior executive jobs in industry and fail.

Organizational cultures directly affect leadership, and it is a mistake for individuals to believe that if they are successful in one culture, they will automatically be successful in another. Leadership in government is in itself a very special process, and therefore, the focus of this book is on government leadership. Our focus is not simply on "administrative" leadership. We are convinced that effective government leaders do not confine themselves to a small administrative box, but rather that leadership in the twenty-first century requires government leaders to be responsible for processes and activities beyond their normal boundaries. Changes in government are forcing its leaders to rethink their role in leadership. We believe a new set of leadership principles is required for success in establishing new leadership roles.

GOVERNMENT AND INDUSTRY: A SIMILAR LEADERSHIP CRISIS

In the 1950s, the United States was responsible for more than 70 percent of all goods and services in the entire world. There was little competition. Consequently, the aim of industry was to produce products and services quickly, since there were ready-made markets throughout the world.

American success can directly be attributed to the ability of business and industry to comprehend and implement the principles of scientific management. Scientific management is a very rational approach, based on time and motion studies, division of labor, individual competition, and individual incentives. Management, by assigning workers tasks, by measuring the time it took the worker to complete a task and the effort taken, could structure and design jobs to maximize individual productivity. The model assumed that if the job was structured and designed correctly, and the worker did as he was told, organizations would be productive. Furthermore, to maximize productivity, the worker would be given financial incentives, and those individuals who out-performed other workers would be rewarded.

Leaders in American industry were quick to employ the scientific model. It worked very well, and this model continues to work extremely well. The United States is still the most productive country in the world.

Government leaders also accepted the scientific management model. Like its industry, the U.S. Government became the most productive government in the world. In our opinion, it would have become even more productive had government been allowed to implement performance incentives. When we tested an individual bonus system within the Department of Labor and Employment Security in Florida, we found a dramatic increase in productivity. Workers within the department were allowed to earn up to $2,300 a year in an individual productivity bonus if they were able to significantly increase their productivity. For most state employees, increasing their productivity, in some cases doubling and tripling productivity, was easy to accomplish.

However, problems remained, and increased productivity was not the answer.

We learned the same lesson that American industry had learned in the latter part of the twentieth century—a successful organization cannot focus only on outputs. For years, government organizations have increased their outputs assuming that if they increased outputs, they would receive more inputs. For example, if the objective is to return people with disabilities to work, and you exceed your quota, you could then request from Congress and the legislature that more inputs (resources) were now needed. The role of the bottom of the organization was to exceed objectives, and the role of the leadership was to successfully argue for more resources.

American industrial leaders managed their organizations similarly. They focused on output. They would also argue for more inputs (resources) when they exceeded their objectives. Most divisions within large corporations were able to successfully negotiate more resources annually. They needed more resources to hire more people and to strengthen their divisions. Consequently, practically every task—engineering, marketing, manufacturing, quality assurance, administrative support, etc.—expanded its specific function. For example, designing an automobile, a process that once was accomplished in less than two years, grew to take as much as seven years during the 1970s. Costs were exorbitant, and waste was plentiful, even in the best U.S. companies such as General Motors, Ford, Xerox, IBM, Motorola, Caterpillar, General Electric, etc. Although government organizations are frequently criticized for waste, business organizations were equally wasteful throughout this period. It was a time of great prosperity in our country, and most leaders, whether they were in government or business, took the position that productivity was the only goal and that the biggest problem was the cost of labor. Many leaders thought that if they could drive down labor costs, then everything would be OK. Very few people took the position that we needed to rethink our management systems, that we needed to rethink how we structure our organizations, that we needed to rethink our attitude toward the American worker, that we needed to rethink how we budget our resources, and that we needed to rethink our organizational focus.

AWAKENING THE GIANT: FOREIGN COMPETITION AND CHANGING CUSTOMERS' WANTS AND NEEDS

In the 1970s when there were significant changes in the U.S. economy, (high inflation, high food and gas prices, etc.), American consumers began to demand more from the products and services they purchased. They did not want just a car, an appliance, a TV, etc.—they wanted quality. They wanted a product that would last, a product that was economical, or a service that satisfied them.

While American organizations continued to design and build products and services that top management thought would sell, foreign competitors were focusing on customer quality, and not just on production. Consumers were demanding quality and cared very little about where products originated. They were far more concerned about the benefits they would derive from their purchases.

In the 1980s, American industries began to understand that they had to change their management methods. Many American organizations embraced Total Quality Management. Those that did quickly realized that it was one thing to embrace TQM and another to implement it. The historically accepted approach of structuring the organization into separate functions and assigning each worker a task had been so embedded that it was very difficult to change. For example, business organizations traditionally divided functions into engineering, manufacturing, quality assurance, delivery, marketing, finance, human resources, information systems, etc. Engineering would design something, pass it on to manufacturing, who would build it, pass it on to quality assurance, who would inspect it and often rebuild it, and pass it on to marketing, who would sell it. If the product didn't meet or exceed the expectations of the customer or didn't sell, each of the divisions (functions) would blame the other.

American industry learned that to achieve success, it could not proceed with a productivity model governed by the principles of scientific management. The old model yielded productivity, but it wasn't just a product that the customer wanted. Consumers wanted a product that worked the first time, every time. They were not willing to invest in just a product, but rather they demanded quality. Consumer needs and wants changed dramatically in the 1980s, forcing industry to change their approach to management. Quality leaders such as Robert Galvin at Motorola, Jack Welch at General Electric, and Lee Iacocca at Chrysler understood the need to change and were willing to take the risk of empowering frontline workers. These leaders, along with thousands of others in industry, recognized the need for change and accepted the challenge.

Furthermore, these leaders understood the new role of the leader in the organization—to empower the work force.

THE AWAKENING OF GOVERNMENT LEADERS

Government organizations are experiencing the same consumer reaction as American industry did. Consumers want and expect more from government services. Consequently, government leaders recognize that they can no longer ignore the American consumer. They can no longer expect to achieve customer satisfaction through the continual use of the scientific management model. Government must change the way it conducts its business. New directions for leadership are required.

Government leaders can no longer perceive their role as being only administrators, but must see themselves as leaders of change. Their job is to transform government organizations from concentrating only on outputs (productivity) to emphasizing quality organizations that focus on meeting or exceeding customer expectations. This is "Transformational Leadership," the focus of this book.

TRANSFORMATIONAL LEADERSHIP DEFINED

Traditional models of leadership primarily focus on getting followers to want to do what leaders want them to do. In other words, the leader knows what is best—the right thing to do in each situation. Success in government (achieving quality), however, is not a matter of telling followers what to do and getting them to do it, but rather enabling individuals and teams to act in the best interest of the organization.

Transformational leadership is defined as a process of inspiring change and empowering followers to achieve greater heights, to improve themselves and to improve organization processes. It is an enabling process causing followers to accept responsibility and accountability for themselves and the processes to which they are assigned.

TRANSFORMATIONAL LEADERSHIP PRINCIPLES

Just as the American consumer forced industry to change, the American taxpayer is demanding that government organizations change. Congress and state legislatures are feeling the pressure from their constituents to "fix" government. Anyone, however, who has had experience in government organizations knows that elected officials are not in the best position to "fix" government. What changed American industrial organization was not the board of directors. They often did not know what to do.

What changed American industry was leadership and the empowerment of the front-line worker. The same applies to government organizations. Tinkering or making dramatic changes in Medicaid, Medicare, welfare, etc. legislation may redirect resources, but the problems of waste, efficiency, effectiveness, and consumer satisfaction will be the responsibility of government leaders. We believe that if government is to achieve efficiency, effectiveness, and consumer and taxpayer respect, it can only be done by professional leaders in government. In other words, government leaders must accept the responsibility for the management of their organization.

It will not be the state legislatures or members of Congress who will make government effective, but rather dedicated and sincere leaders who put the needs of the people they serve above their own self-interest. It will take government leaders who are willing to step out, be proactive, and take the lead in reducing waste and improving their organizations to meet consumer demands, rather than administering programs for their convenience and personal ambitions. It will require government leaders to adopt a new set of leadership principles. These principles will require government leaders not just to serve the needs of elected officials, but rather to serve the people they manage and their customers. To become transformational leaders, we suggest that government leaders adopt the following transformational leadership principles.

Principles of Transformational Leadership

PRINCIPLE #1: View organizations as systems.

Traditional government managers frequently view organizations as separate and distinct functions. Their concept of organization is a simple one. Work is divided into functions, and within each function is a distinct division of labor among employees. The job of the leader in a traditionally managed organization is to direct the labor force to fulfill the purpose of each function and concentrate on the performance of individuals.

Transformational leaders, on the other hand, view the organization as a system that is composed of interrelationships and interactions among employees to achieve specified organizational outcomes. Transformational leaders perceive their role as improving processes so they can deliver value to their customers. They organize their organization not around functions, but around processes with the focus on delivering value to customers. Their goal is to develop and implement efficient and effective management systems. To be efficient means to minimize waste in transforming inputs into outputs. Effective means to provide outputs that yield desired outcomes for government customers.

Government leaders should not make the mistake of following traditional industrial leadership models, since most traditional leadership models focus only on outputs when they define effectiveness. Government is very unique in that results are far more related to outcomes than outputs. For example, Peter Drucker claims that "there is only one valid definition of the goal of business: to create customers." In government, the goal is often just the opposite—reduction of customers. If you are the leader of a welfare organization, your goal should not be to issue more welfare checks (create new customers), but rather to issue fewer (reduce your customer base). One of the most serious problems of government leadership is that leaders will actually foster the need for welfare payments (services), since that will increase the size and the need for their organization. If government leadership was truly or ideally effective, in many cases, the goal would be to put their organization out of business.

The new leader in government will *not* try to increase power by developing large organizations, but will work toward a reduction in the need for services. Such leaders view themselves from a systems perspective.

Adopting a systems perspective will force leaders to change their approach from one that just reacts to legislation and problems of administering legislative intent, to a proactive leadership approach that focuses on customer outcomes and on continually improving processes. Transformational leaders view the organization from a total systems perspective.

PRINCIPLE #2: *Establish and communicate organization strategy.*

What is the best use of organization resources? How does one go about deploying these resources? In developing organizational strategy, these two questions must be answered. Leaders are responsible for developing, implementing, and communicating strategy. In government, strategy means the organization's plan for achieving desirable outcomes. Transformational leaders work with others to create the vision, the mission, the values, the design of the organization, the structures, goals, and the use of human resources. Strategy should not be a well-kept secret, but should be shared with all members of the organization.

PRINCIPLE #3: *Institutionalize a management system.*

Traditionally, managers in government have been able to elect their own management system. This is acceptable when functions are divided and there is a division of labor. However, it is unacceptable when organizations are viewed as systems. When organizations are viewed as systems, a management system that everyone in the organization uses should be implemented. It is very difficult, and practically impossible, to empower associates to improve systems throughout the organization if varying sets of management beliefs and principles are employed by managers.

PRINCIPLE #4: *Develop and train all associates in process management.*

Traditionally, organizations have offered management training to managers and skill training to others in the organization. Managers were taught the principles of planning, organizing, directing, and controlling, while other associates were trained to perform their tasks more effectively. Transformational leaders expect associates to use their brains to improve processes. Therefore, managers and associates receive similar training. Both managers and associates are responsible for improving processes and need to grow so that they can effectively improve their processes. Training may be required in the areas of customer focus, data collection and analysis, team development, flowcharting, etc. Training and development is not for just a select few, but is required of all associates.

PRINCIPLE #5: Empower individuals and teams.

Rather than directing subordinates by telling them what to do, transformational leaders transfer their power to members of their organization so that associates not only accept the responsibility for improving organizational processes, but also have the authority to take action they feel is in the best interest of the organization. Traditional administrators in government often find the empowerment issue of associates very difficult to accept. They mistakenly believe that if associates are empowered, they are given the right to do whatever they feel like doing. That perhaps might be the case if one applied empowerment in the traditional management approach. However, trained associates, whose task it is to improve organizational processes in a systematic approach using scientific methods, clearly understand their boundaries and role in decision making. For the most part, associates' actions are governed by team consensus and organizational values. Furthermore, transformational leaders don't have to use their time and effort to control the behavior of their associates, but rather can control the processes for which they are responsible. Transformational leaders manage and control processes allowing associates the freedom to select behaviors that they believe are appropriate for contributing to continual improvement, whether they act individually or within a team.

PRINCIPLE #6: Measure and control prcesses.

Traditional administrators focus primarily on assigned functions and division of labor. They primarily measure only outputs and individual productivity. Transformational leaders, on the other hand, measure inputs, process activities, outputs, and outcomes. They focus daily on quality indicators and data collected at specific points within the process to maintain control.

PRINCIPLE #7: Recognize and reward continual improvement.

Effective traditional administrators understood the importance of recognition and rewards. They were always anxious to somehow reward those who were outstanding in their performance. However, even the best administrators often found it difficult to properly reward those who did an outstanding job because other workers in the office rarely understood why they were not selected. When one individual is recognized above all others, jealousy can often consume their peers. The recognition of one individual may thus produce unhealthy competition rather than cooperation.

Transformational leaders recognize continual improvement first, and those who contribute toward making continual improvements in their process are then recognized. The best approach to motivation is to let teams recognize individuals and let leaders recognize and reward teams. Transformational leaders build recognition and reward systems that focus on teams, and furthermore, praise teams who take the time and the risk to recognize and reward one of their own.

PRINCIPLE #8: Inspire continual change.

Traditional administrators often resist change since they believe their job is to control their subordinates. It is much easier to control subordinates when the climate is very stable. Subordinates know what is expected of them, and their jobs do not change. Transformational leaders, on the other hand, understand that continual improvement is necessary just to maintain gains. There is hardly a job that exists today which exists as it did five years ago. It is easy to understand, for example, that professionals who don't improve themselves will not be able to maintain the gains they made in their profession only a few years ago. The same applies to systems in organizations. With the advancement of technology and product development, organizational systems change rapidly just to maintain the effectiveness their systems achieved only a few years ago. Transformational leaders know that it is their responsibility to cause change. The role of a transformational leader is to inspire others to continually improve themselves and organizational processes. Rather than resisting change, such leaders embrace change and employ change strategies to improve the organization.

ORGANIZATION OF THIS BOOK

This book is designed to assist the reader to develop and use the transformational leadership principles outlined above. It describes what is required to be a transformational leader, what is required to develop these principles, and how to implement these principles in a government organization. We believe that government leadership is the key to making government efficient and effective. Government leaders can no longer perceive themselves as administrators, but rather must see themselves as leaders of change who are willing to take the risk of empowering associates to achieve desirable organizational outcomes.

In the next chapter, we will describe the development of the "systems thinking" necessary to empower others. Then, in Chapter 3, we discuss the required elements of an empowerment organization including vision, mission, values, strategic plans, and outcomes. In Chapter 4, transformational leadership characteristics are defined, and in Chapter 5, the required leadership skills are presented. In Chapter 6, our focus will be on transformational leadership behaviors, followed by a description of transformational leadership substitutes in Chapter 7. In Chapter 8, we will discuss how transformational leaders inspire continual improvement and innovation.

CHAPTER 2

EMPOWERING SYSTEMS

The concept of "empowerment" is one frequently found in organizational literature and frequently discussed in management circles. Although empowerment appears to be an easy concept to discuss and define, it is seldom fully employed by practicing administrators. In fact, traditional administrators often think of empowerment as being idealistic and think of empowerment as a fad. Administrators who have accepted the empowerment concept and believe in its usefulness in developing effective and efficient organizations often find it extremely difficult to implement, something which is quite frustrating to administrators who attempt to implement the concept. It is practically impossible to empower subordinates when one works in an organization that practices traditional government administration.

We believe that one cannot successfully empower subordinates in a vacuum. An organization must be designed to empower all associates. To achieve maximum results that can be obtained from empowering associates, a systems approach should be implemented throughout the organization. Empowerment requires administrators in government to practice leadership at all levels and to incorporate systems thinking, rather than viewing the organization in terms of functions and silos.

GOVERNMENT ORGANIZATIONS AS SYSTEMS

A system is an arrangement of things that are related or connected to form a unified or organic whole. As a concept, "systems" are easily understood. For example, it is relatively easy to comprehend the human body as a system composed of subsystems, such as the circulatory or digestive system. Also, it is relatively easy to understand an irrigation system, or for that matter the solar system. Furthermore, it is relatively easy to comprehend organizations as systems when they are described as such. However, when individuals take a position within a large system, they tend to narrow their perspective from thinking about the organization as a complete system to thinking about the task to which they are assigned. They frequently do not think of their work outside of the boundaries of their assigned jobs. Furthermore, when individuals become promoted to administrators in government, they still confine their thinking to the functions for which they are now accountable. Rather than viewing the organization as a system, administrators frequently fall into the trap of viewing the organization from a functional perspective. They perceive their job as an administrator to be confined within a narrow set of parameters. Consequently, you will often hear administrators say, "that is not the responsibility of my department," when a problem emerges. Administrators who think functionally often criticize other functions in the organizations for being ineffective and are quick to defend the effectiveness of their function when the overall results of the organization are not acceptable.

Government administrators can no longer take the position that they are effective leaders if they are successful (in their perception) managing their assigned functions, while the organization fails to achieve desirable outcomes. Even though effective administrators are not responsible for the entire system, they must enlarge their boundaries, think beyond their functions, and concern themselves with a relationship of their work to other components of the organization. Leadership in the twenty-first century requires all leaders to have a holistic perspective of the organization. They must think "outside of the box" and influence others to see their organization, not from a single-task perspective, but rather as interconnected processes. When unified, these processes form a system that delivers desirable outcomes.

We learned in the latter half of the twentieth century that dividing work and functions increased productivity but did not, in many cases, deliver desirable outcomes. For example, automobile manufacturers recruited some of the most competent design engineers, had elaborate manufacturing technology, had highly paid and sophisticated management, etc., and yet were unable to deliver what the customer desired. Their failure was not attributed to laziness or lack of resources, but rather to an ineffective system. Managers frequently thought that their job was to meet their assigned objectives, and therefore treated their function in isolation. What management couldn't see was that even if each function met it's objectives, the organization could fail. For example, design engineers would meet their objectives of designing a car. They then would pass it on to manufacturing, whose job was to figure out how to build it. When manufacturing complained that the design had many flaws, the design engineers would argue that the design was acceptable, but that the people in manufacturing were incompetent. Manufacturing would do the best they could and pass it on to quality assurance, who would shake their heads and rework the product in order to meet the objectives of delivering the automobile on time.

The cost of manufacturing a car using the functional approach was excessive and had to be passed on to the consumer. When the marketing functional unit tested the car with customers, they began complaining that the car was not what the consumer wanted. Top management in the automobile industry insisted that marketing achieve its sales objectives, or they would find replacements to do the job. The marketing department then went to work and, in order to be successful, had to compensate the consumer in one form or another in order to get them to purchase the automobile. For example, they came up with extended warranty plans, factory discounts, and extended credit plans.

Of course, all of this added cost to the car and lost revenue for the automobile manufacturer. Since foreign competitors had figured out a better management system than the functional approach, thousands of jobs were lost. Ford Motor Company, for example, went from 200,000 employees in January 1979 to 86,000 employees by July 1, 1980.

Thus we learned a very valuable but costly lesson—that the system is the problem. An effective system is required to achieve desirable results.

If government organizations are to achieve efficiency and effectiveness, administrators will have to become leaders, and take the position that they can no longer think and act functionally, can no longer merely pass the results on to the next department and expect it to correct their mistakes, but must adopt a systems perspective and think of the organization holistically.

EMPOWERING ORGANIZATIONS

Empowerment is difficult to achieve in isolation. Organizational systems are just as important as leadership. Moving from a functional, independent, organizational structure to an interrelated system is a requirement for organizations that desire an empowered work force. Many government administrators believe, and will hold to the belief, that their job is to give orders and that the job of their subordinates is to follow them. In today's organizational environment, there are many emerging leaders who are becoming increasingly frustrated with administrators who cling to traditional administration. These new leaders wonder how the old administrators can believe that the outpouring of criticism by taxpayers and customers will soon pass and that there is no need to change.

In a seminar sponsored by the Federal Quality Institute, Vice President Al Gore communicated his sense of frustration in trying to influence government administrators to change their approach to management. He learned that changing organizations, especially embedded bureaucracies, is not something that can be accomplished in three or four years. Gore also advocated radical changes in government; however, from our experience we believe the best approach to change is incremental change. Incremental change is more logical, more enduring, and more effective. Radical change is required when the system has completely failed or technology has been developed to the point where it can replace a process.

Empowering organizations are built upon four cornerstones: process oriented, customer focused, data driven, and team based. Furthermore, they adopt and practice a set of beliefs and principles which promote the use of associates' brain power for the purpose of continually improving organization processes. Empowerment is not something that an administrator delegates or grants to associates by allowing them to do whatever they want to do. Rather it begins with organizations designing, developing, and implementing systems that are conducive to empowerment. Without focusing first on systems, empowerment is likely to fail.

CORNERSTONES AND BELIEFS OF EMPOWERING ORGANIZATIONS

Organizations that empower their work forces build their foundations on four cornerstones: process orientation, customer focus, data-driven decisions, and team-based continual process improvement. We believe that the cornerstones anchor empowerment philosophy. They are interrelated and together provide the foundation for an empowering system.

1. Process orientation.

Fundamental to empowerment is that organizations organize around processes and manage their processes. Traditional organizations, on the other hand, organize around functions and manage people. It is imperative to understand that over 90 percent of improvements in organization stem from improving processes. In other words, the best method for improving the performance of associates is to improve organization processes. People in organizations generally fail when their processes fail. Organizations that experience poor results frequently show that in 85 to 90 percent of the time, the associates were doing what they were supposed to do. Prior to the quality movement, organizations that were experiencing poor performance were unable to explain why 90 percent of their employees were rated by their supervisors as meeting or exceeding supervisory expectations. In fact, one of the authors was a consultant in the 1970s to a major corporation that decided to get tough on employee evaluations. Every manager ranked the performance of their subordinates and were asked to terminate the lower one-third. Even after trimming out the "dead weight," the organization still experienced poor results. It wasn't until the middle 1980s that they were able to figure out that it wasn't the employees who were the problem, but rather the functionally designed system.

Organizing work around processes requires the organization to flowchart it's core processes. A flowchart should be prepared which graphically displays the core processes of the organization. For example, in Florida's Department of Labor and Employment Security, we were able to define six core processes that explained how work flows within the six divisions in the department. These core processes were:

- rehabilitation

- jobs, benefits, and appeals

- prevention, regulation, and protection

- collection, analysis, and dissemination of workforce information

- revenue collection

- administrative support

We define a process as a series of steps that we perform to produce a product or service. A process includes input, process activities, outputs, and outcomes. To properly flowchart a process, one can begin with a supplier or with the customer and work backwards. An example of a process follows.

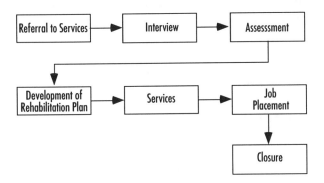

This flowchart is a very simple example, with almost every activity box actually a process that should be examined independently. For example, the "Interview" actually contains a series of steps that undoubtedly contain a number of decision points that would be shown with a "diamond" shaped box.

Once processes are clearly defined, leaders and associates work closely together to improve process performance. Without clearly delineating processes, there is very little need for empowerment because associates will be in a quandary as to their job expectations. On the other hand, with processes clearly defined, associates understand that they are empowered to test and implement changes that improve the processes to which they are assigned. There is no end to the process of improvement. A fundamental principle in a team-based, empowering organization is that every process can be improved again and again.

Empowering organizations function with open systems. This means they go beyond the traditional boundaries. Their processes include suppliers, customers, and partners. In government, the suppliers often include referral agencies, the vendors that supply services, and may include employers who seek individuals who have progressed through the department's processes. Each of these suppliers has a vital interest in the success of the customer's program, and each shares the benefits resulting in quality services. At the other end of the process are customers who receive products. It is critical that customer's needs and expectations are measured through a variety of ways, including surveys, focus groups, etc.

Partners may include the state legislature, the Governor, the federal government, comptroller, auditor general, federal inspectors, and unions. Each of these has an interest in the organization's success with customers and shares responsibility in the development of an empowering organization focused on quality and customer satisfaction.

2. Customer focus.

Focusing on the customer is one of the more difficult transitions for government workers to make. Traditionally, government personnel are expected to meet objectives and quotas. Consequently, it has been ingrained into government personnel that if they meet objectives and quotas, they are successful. However, in an empowerment system, the customer comes first. Objectives and quotas become a by-product of work and meeting or exceeding customer expectations is the goal. Many government administrators argue that the results of their work frequently make people unhappy and therefore, they would be counterproductive to focus on their happiness. This is no doubt true and therefore, one must understand that customer focus does not mean customer service. Customer focus means directing efforts towards meeting or exceeding customer expectations. It does not mean that every customer becomes a happy customer. It does mean, though, that you meet or exceed their expectations.

For example, a person speeding down the highway might be unhappy to receive a ticket, but the police officer exceeded their expectations by catching them speeding. We exceed people's expectations when we catch them trying to receive two or three extra welfare checks or unemployment benefits. On the other hand, we exceed customer expectations when they expected to spend three or four hours waiting to be processed for a government benefit, and then find they only have to wait fifteen minutes. We meet customer expectations when they receive their benefits on time and for the correct amount. We meet or exceed their expectations when we are able to help them find a job when they are unemployed. We meet or exceed their expectations when they are able to read, write, and do math at the twelfth grade level when they graduate from high school.

We have all witnessed how frustrated some front-line workers in government organizations become when they are serving customers. We watched workers in a large metropolitan office who were trained in customer service and knew how to be friendly and respectable to customers. We found that what frustrated them the most was that they knew more than ten percent of their customers would not be processed accurately or on time. They knew that many of their customers were going to have to call the "800" number to find out what went wrong with their application. In fact, in one study over 90 percent of the government customers were standing in line to correct errors made in the system that could have been avoided in a financial aid office. It was understandable why the people working in this area did everything they could to avoid direct contact with the customer.

Leaders in government organizations can no longer sit behind their desks and ignore customers. It is no wonder why there are so many levels of management in government organizations. Government bureaucrats spend most of their time hiding from customers and building practically invincible forts to avoid contact with customers. Everyone in the organization, from top to bottom, must understand that they must focus on the customer if they are to achieve quality. Rather than always looking to administrators for what objectives to achieve and how to do their jobs, government personnel should focus on their customers. The reason they are motivated to improve their processes is not because they want top administrators to look good, but because they want to provide the highest quality service to their customers. One of the primary reasons government is able to attract quality people is because many individuals are motivated to serve their country and community. In other words, they care. Providing associates with the opportunity to demonstrate they care daily is one of the positive outcomes of allowing them to improve processes that ultimately meet or exceed customer expectations.

3. Data-driven decisions.

Traditional administrators for years have known the importance of data. In fact, most government organizations collect more data and perhaps use it less than anyone else. The problem for most government agencies is that even though they collect much data, very little of it is meaningful and used for effective decision making. Most government data is used to establish objectives. It is also used to substantiate how effective the organization has been and to persuade Congress and state legislatures that the organization could even do better if it had more resources. Traditional organizations seldom share information with front-line worker, and seldom use it to improve processes.

Data, however, is a cornerstone for empowerment organizations since the driving force for improving processes stems from collected and analyzed data. Associates cannot be empowered to improve processes if timely, accurate, and meaningful data is not available on how well the process is working. Therefore, empowered associates understand and use appropriate tools and methods for data collection and analysis. Collecting data is a daily activity and having associates proficient in data collection and analysis is a requirement for empowering systems.

4. Team-based continual process improvement.

For years bureaucracies have employed administrative theories that have called for the division of labor, rules and regulations, hierarchy of authority, unity of command, and discipline. The concept was a simple one—if you can control individuals, then you can control productivity. Thus, by assigning a person a task and telling the person what to do and how to do it, administrators would be successful.

In empowering organizations, leaders ask much more from associates. They ask them not to work independently, but to work in teams. We believe that collaborative efforts are far more effective than individuals working alone. Therefore, individuals are assigned to teams which are held accountable for an assigned process or processes. The team is responsible for flowcharting their processes, collecting and analyzing data, and coming up with solutions that improve their assigned process. Since each process has a supplier and a customer, the team works closely with their suppliers and is constantly monitoring their customers to see how well their process is doing in meeting and/or exceeding customer expectations. Teams insure that they have valid answers to questions such as who the customers are of their program, why customers need their service, what customers expect from their process, how customers benefit from their service, or what legal, budget, or technological restraints impact customer service.

EMPOWERING SYSTEMS BELIEFS

Traditional organizations seldom adopted a set of beliefs. Each administrator was allowed to bring into the organization a personal set of beliefs about people and organizations. It wasn't uncommon for two managers working in the same unit to have diametrically opposed convictions about human behavior. For example, administrator "A" might believe that people are basically lazy and inherently dislike work. Therefore, "A" thought the best way to motivate subordinates was to coerce them and control them. On the other hand, administrator "B" believed that most people naturally enjoyed expending physical and mental energy and were committed to work. Administrator "B" took the position that, if you involve subordinates in goal setting, they will exercise self-direction and seek responsibility. They believed their subordinates were creative, industrious and appreciated the opportunity to exercise their brains on the job.

Empowering systems promote a belief system that is organization-wide, and expect leaders to adopt their beliefs. Organizations with very strong cultures can affect individual beliefs. Over time organizational beliefs can positively influence individuals as they learn to cope with everyday problems in the organization. By observing others, individuals learn that there is a pattern of behavior that is acceptable and unacceptable. In organizations where there is a weak culture, individuals have more freedom to choose values, beliefs and assumptions. We believe that effective organizations have strong cultures and encourage associates to share a similar belief system.

Empowerment organizations, for example, should not recruit or promote administrators who hold beliefs contrary to the beliefs of the organization. Critics might argue this is an unhealthy activity, since you want to recruit a diversified work force. On the contrary, organizations that adopt a strong belief system and expect organizational members to adopt it are more likely to attract a diversified work force. Discriminating on the basis of beliefs fundamental to the organization does not mean you exclude people on the basis of their education, race, nationality, etc. Rather you are asking people who join your organization to share a conviction about concepts fundamental to organizational effectiveness.

Traditional administrators focus on controlling people and therefore, recruit and promote people who exhibit behaviors that they find controllable. Therefore, many people from different walks of life, with different nationalities, race and lifestyles are excluded. None of the aforementioned affect organizational outcomes. On the other hand, people who espouse beliefs that are contrary to making the organization successful can have a very negative affect on outcomes. To achieve diversity, quality and desirable outcomes, organizations should adopt a set of beliefs that empower their work force. We believe that the following set of beliefs promote and instill empowerment.

BELIEFS

1. Organization-wide commitment, involvement and principles.

Organizations are complete systems. Functions cannot be viewed in isolation, but rather treated as processes and are interrelated. The philosophies and practices within the organization are organization-wide. Everyone is involved and is committed. Everyone receives similar training. Everyone understands the overall mission of the organization, the strategy and the approach. Everyone, from top to bottom, embraces the cornerstones, the beliefs, the values and the guiding principles of the organization. Quality is not delegated, but is everyone's responsibility.

2. Prevention, not detection, is the best strategy.

Traditional government organizations have largely focused on detection as one of its best practices. Al Gore once commented that one out of three people in government is watching the other two. It seems like every day in the newspaper, auditors in state government detect waste in government. Furthermore, government personnel spend an inordinate amount of time detecting and correcting errors. Process improvement team members in government, when flowcharting their processes, are often amazed to see how much time is spent correcting errors occurring in a prior process supplied by others. It is discouraging that others would send their work forward knowing that there were probably errors in their work. When we would ask specific personnel why they sent the work forward, the common answer was they had a quota to fill each day. Finally, we were amazed at how many people working in government routinely accepted poor quality work, and thought it was part of their job to detect and correct errors.

Empowerment systems hold the belief that the most effective and economical method is to do the work right the first time, prevent errors, and not pass along poor quality work. One of the primary reasons to empower your work force is to give them the authority and responsibility to improve the system and to prevent errors and problems. One of the goals of government organizations should be to eliminate the need for auditors by developing "foolproof systems." In other words, processes that are so effective, any fool could not make mistakes. To achieve this goal, all government personnel must believe that their job is to prevent, not detect and correct errors.

3. People are untapped resources.

Frequently administrators complain that their organization would function more effectively if they were able to hire better people. Many of them have the attitude that people are the problem, and not the system. These same administrators hold the belief that people working for them are very limited, are actually stupid, and whatever opinion or suggestion they might make is of little value. Obviously, if an administrator holds this belief then they would not want to empower employees.

Transformational leaders, on the other hand, believe that people are untapped resources. No matter what their position, their title, their educational background, nationality, race or lifestyle, everyone can be a vital resource for the organization. They believe that when people are armed with facts and data and involved in decision making, they will do the right thing. People are an extraordinary resource, and it is their brain power that transformational leaders know that they must tap.

4. Continual improvement is required.

For the past several decades, both business and government organizations have stressed innovation, and not continual improvement. Most of these organizations emphasize "the great-leap approach." Heroes in organizations were people who focused on developing technological breakthroughs. They searched for dramatic new ways of doing things. Rather than focusing on small steps to improve organization, they looked for ways to make great leaps. The great-leap approach is still in vogue and can be observed by following those in government who have attached themselves to the concept of reinventing government. Many advocates of reinventing government believe that the answer to government ills can be found by a select group of people in Washington, or in a state capital, overhauling government operations.

Transformational leaders do not just worship at the alter of innovation, but rather believe that the best approach to improving government is to continually improve government processes. While innovation and reinvention are often very expensive and call for a large investment, continual improvement is essentially free since it's philosophy can be easily incorporated into the daily activities of government personnel.

Since all systems deteriorate over time, continual improvement is required just to maintain the gains. That in itself is sufficient to adopt the belief that continual improvement is a requirement. However, adopting the continual improvement philosophy can yield remarkable results. Although government organizations have typically recognized and given much fanfare to people who achieve striking breakthroughs, most real gains in improvement in organizations evolve from people who incrementally improve the way work flows. Innovation will always play a significant role in the advancement of government organizations, but continual improvement is the most effective strategy. Transformational leaders embrace continual improvement and expect others to believe that incremental change, taking small steps, is the best approach to improving organizations.

5. People closest to process are in the best position to improve it.

Traditionally government administrators believe that solutions to organizational problems belong only to management. From time to time, effective administrators would establish a committee, composed of some of their bright subordinates, to advise them on what could be done to solve a specific problem (management by participation). The purpose of these committees was to advise management, and members of the committee were not empowered to solve problems. Nor should they have been empowered, since most committees worked in functional units and were not aware of how changing work in one unit affected a process in another. Only managers were expected to understand the larger picture.

Furthermore, many effective administrators became frustrated when they found a better way to improve work, but had to ask permission from those above them to implement the change. The request for change often required the preparation of a formal document and might take weeks or even months to get a response. In one case, for example, an administrator generated five specific recommendations in a formal document to his supervisor. The recommendations sat on the supervisor's desk for over a month before he finally sent them up the chain of command (i.e., the "black hole in the sky"). Eight and a half months later, after a number of inquiries, the administrator advocating the change finally received a response that suggested that he wait until after "the new legislation was approved." He could then submit his recommendations if they were still appropriate. This is not an uncommon situation. Many people working in government have given up trying to suggest improvements.

Organizations that believe in empowerment realize that the best source for improvement are people closely connected to the processes. These individuals thoroughly understand the processes to which they are assigned, and are in the best position to look for root causes to solve and prevent problems. When we empowered front-line workers in Florida's Department of Labor and Employment Security, we were able to significantly reduce our error rate and customer waiting time by allowing front-line associates to make changes in the process. These individuals understood the work, could flowchart the process accurately, and were able to develop improvements.

6. Beliefs and values drive organizational behavior.

Many government bureaucracies rely heavily on rules to control organizational behavior. Rules evolve over the years as a form of communication to organizational members regarding what they can and cannot do. Traditional administrators believed that if every member followed the rules, the organization would be successful. The problem with rules is that one cannot write a sufficient number of rules to govern all behavior. For example, one division had a rule that a front-line worker could not spend more than twelve minutes with each customer. Of course, this rule had to be broken frequently. Then the rule was changed, and it required that front-line workers had to average twelve minutes per customer. Therefore, if they went over five minutes with one customer, they had to make it up with another customer. With a rule like this, it is easy to understand why the error rate was so high and why customer surveys indicated so much dissatisfaction.

A more effective method of governing behavior is to establish and communicate the beliefs and values of the organization throughout the organization. Beliefs establish the convictions of the organization, and values guide behavior. They explain "what ought to be." Empowering systems rely on beliefs and values to drive behavior in the organization. They make the assumption that if beliefs and values are firmly embedded in every member, they will be able to select the correct behavior for each situation. In the next chapter we will discuss values in more detail and will give as an example the values adopted by Florida's Department of Labor and Employment Security.

SUMMARY

To be a successful government leader, an empowering system must be developed and maintained. Transformational leaders accept and support the following transformational leadership principles:

1. View and understand government organizations as systems.

2. Adopt the cornerstones and beliefs of empowerment organizations.

CHAPTER 3

TRANSFORMATIONAL LEADERSHIP: VISION AND STRATEGY

Transformational leadership requires the leader to influence others to accept responsibility for making decisions that improve organizational processes. Unlike traditional approaches to leadership where leaders seek approval for a predetermined decision, the objective of transformational leadership is to get others to do the right thing the first time. Transformational leaders are expected to set the stage for continual improvement. They influence others to help them create an environment or culture that promotes continual improvement and associate empowerment.

CREATE A VISION FOR THE ORGANIZATION

Transformational leadership begins with a vision. Leaders answer the question, "what do I want to create?" Great leaders, such as Kennedy, Churchill, Gandhi, and King all had a vision of where they wanted to lead their followers. Exceptional business leaders such as Watson at IBM, Welch at General Electric, and Iacocca at Chrysler all began with a vision. They knew where they wanted their organizations to be in the future.

It is far more difficult for government administrators to visualize greatness for their organization. To begin with, elected officials like to believe that they are "the visionaries" and that appointed government leaders are the administrators. As we walked the halls of Congress and attended legislative meetings, it was clear to us that elected officials felt they were superior and had solutions to government problems. As appointed government leaders, our job was to listen, answer questions when asked, and "kiss up" to them because they controlled the resources.

The hypocritical nature of elected officials became quite apparent to us. They were elected because they were supposedly the best representatives of the voting public. Yet, the constituents they served often came in second to their personal need for power. For example, if they got angry with a government administrator, they would punish the individual by withdrawing their support and resources for the administrator's department. It did not make any difference that the constituents who were served by the appointed official's department suffered because of their actions.

On the other hand, the government administrator often was far more interested in flexing power and playing games with legislators to outwit them. The goal was one of constantly trying to get more resources, i.e., more money and staff, to grow and to offer more services. Their success depended upon the personalities and whims of legislators. Sometimes the officials won, and sometimes they lost, rarely on the merits of what was right for their customers. Consequently, many appointed government leaders often lost their faith in the system. To make matters worse, appointed government administrators felt that they were trapped in whatever vision they inherited in the department that was consistently supported by elected officials.

Twenty-first century government leaders have a new opportunity, and in our opinion, should seize it. They now have a new opportunity to move from being administrators to government leaders, since many elected officials and taxpayers now understand or are beginning to understand that government systems are the problem and can only be fixed by the people who work in them. Just as the board of directors and top management of major industrial organizations learned in the 1970s and 1980s that they needed quality systems to compete with international competitors, so too have many elected officials and taxpayers come to realize that the solutions to effective government rest in government leadership, associates, and quality systems.

Elected officials do not have the answers. In fact, we believe the country would be better served if legislatures only met once every four years so that agency leaders and administrators would understand that they are responsible for vision and strategy. Furthermore, they would not be distracted by elected officials who often do more harm than good.

Let's be realistic. Congress and state legislatures are going to continue to meet and look for solutions. Government leaders, however, need to consider their roles in a new perspective. Rather than blaming our lawmakers, they should accept responsibility for the government organizations they lead. Rather than look to lawmakers for solutions, they should look to their associates for solutions. Their objective should be to improve government systems, and their leadership approach should be to empower associates to "fix" the processes to which they are assigned.

A vision statement encompasses a wide variety of issues and is often very difficult to write. Transformational leaders will have a vision statement and it might include: customers, performance results, use of human resources, style of leadership, use of information and analysis, strategy, and process management and improvement. An example of a vision statement follows:

Vocational Rehabilitation

With our community partners, create an environment in which a continuum of rehabilitation is available for people with disabilities.

The vision statement for the state of Florida might be, "The Best place in the world to live and work."

DEVELOP A MISSION STATEMENT

The fourth step to transformational leadership is to develop a mission. It describes the purpose of the organization. Too many government organizations rely on Congress or state legislators to define their missions. In other words, rather than defining their missions from the customer's perspective, they automatically borrow the language from Congress or their state legislature to define their missions.

Legally, they are correct. However, their organization must fulfill a larger mission in order to be successful. For example, the mission for the Division of Unemployment Compensation might be to process unemployment claims and pay benefits. When we analyzed this mission in the Department of Labor and Employment Security, we realized that if government was to truly serve the taxpayers and their clients, the mission of Unemployment Compensation should be enlarged. The Department's mission was not only just to pay benefits, but to return people to work. Its job was not limited to unemployment claims, but to serve its clientele. Therefore, by enlarging its mission, front-line associates were not only empowered to process claims, but to help their customers obtain a job. When front-line associates interviewed their clients, they were aware of jobs that were available and understood that their goal was not just to pay benefits, but to help their customers find another job.

An important quality indicator for the Division of Unemployment Compensation was to reduce the amount of time an individual spent unemployed. Congress isn't close enough to the customer to understand what the mission of the Division of Unemployment should be. Congress and state legislators often think of organizations only as "silos," and are strong advocates of the division of responsibilities, i.e., one function in each silo. When we worked in the Division of Unemployment Compensation, we did not allow legislators' limited vision to keep us from doing what was right. In a later chapter we will discuss the difficulty of making this transition.

Newspaper journalists and organizational critics often denounce the importance of mission statements. They believe that most mission statements are largely ceremonial and completely detached from employees. We take issue with these critics, and argue that systems designed to empower associates require a clear definition of the purpose of the organization. Mission statements, properly employed, can have a significant impact upon associates. An effective mission statement answers the following questions:

1. Who are we?

2. What is our purpose?

3. For whom do we do it?

4. Why do we do it?

ESTABLISH ORGANIZATION VALUES

The fifth step for transformational leadership is to establish organization values. As noted in the previous chapter, values drive behavior. They signal what is right and how we ought to behave.

We believe that one of the problems of government is that taxpayers and legislators expect government to be run as though it is a business and expect government to adopt business values. Legislators are constantly trying to convert government systems to business systems. Legislators are preoccupied with the bottom-line end and results.

In principle, the ideal goal of any business is to create a monopoly. Government has already achieved this objective. In most cases, government has a monopoly over most services that they provide. Business organizations work hard to retain old customers and create new ones. Government, on the other hand, is often trying to "get rid of" customers in most cases. For example, we do not need more customers for unemployment, welfare, rehabilitation, workers compensation, prisons, disasters, etc. While business organizations work hard to create a monopoly, many government organizations should be working hard to go out of business.

Legislators, having the attitude that government should be managed the same as business, may easily fall in the trap every year of providing more resources to those organizations that create a bigger government by successfully achieving their goals and quotas. It is no wonder government organizations increase in size. They are often managed like a business. If, for example, government organizations that provide welfare did not find more people to provide welfare checks to each year, their organization would get smaller.

It is time for lawmakers to discard their business model and begin seeing government organizations in a new light. It is time for government leaders to adopt a systems approach to government if government is to be successful in the twenty-first century. It will require government leaders to educate lawmakers about government systems and to show them how their leadership and effective organization are the solution to government problems. Establishing a set of values helps guide the behavior in this endeavor.

The following values were established in Florida's Department of Employment Security.

Values

- **Quality**—is meeting customer requirements the first time and every time. Our internal and external customers include individuals, teams, and organizations who receive and use the output of our work process.

- **Responsiveness**—is the willingness and ability to provide information, reply to requests, answer questions, and complete tasks promptly. In order to create and maintain an atmosphere of "total quality," it is necessary to have the ability to respond in a positive and timely manner. With regard to providing quality customer service, it is absolutely essential to meet or exceed the expectations of all customers in terms of responsiveness.

- **Flexibility**—is the ready capability for modification or change, and the adaptability to new situations. Flexibility in the workplace allows for acceptance of change in processes, procedures, and requirements to support the accomplishment of the agency's mission, goals, and objectives in light of an ever-changing environment and the demands of shifting priorities. Continual improvement requires flexibility as positive changes are constantly sought.

- **Respect**—is the quality of accepting and holding in high esteem all persons' rights to their beliefs, values, autonomy, and differences while treating them with dignity, worth, courtesy, civility, and politeness. Respect is the ability to actively listen to others without interruption, prejudice, judgment, or reservation, and is the acknowledgment of the worth of others' time.

- **Sense of Total Commitment**— is carrying out the pledge to do something. Total commitment is awareness of the need to be continuously involved in the activities intended to achieve quality work. Continual improvement is an integral part of our daily operations.

- **Open and Honest Communication**—is an expression of a professional work environment which facilitates the exchange of information, ideas, and divergent opinions between all levels of an organization in an atmosphere of respect and genuine concern for the best interests of the organization, its associates, and customers.

- **Humor**—is a characteristic disposition or state of mind that allows oneself and others a perception of amusement. Non-offensive humor provides a link between individuals and creates unity out of diversity. A shared bit of humor encourages the development of "common ground." It serves to motivate workers to carry on in their jobs despite occasional unpleasantness.

- **Empowerment**—is the freedom and power to act, command, or decide upon a course of action. Teams are empowered with authority related to the work and processes for which they are responsible, in order to achieve gains in quality and productivity.

- **Teamwork**—is the ability of a group of individuals to work together toward a common vision by each doing a part to achieve the efficiency of the whole. It is the capacity to direct individual accomplishment toward organizational objectives. It is the fuel that allows common people to attain uncommon results.

- **People**—We believe that people are intelligent, creative, knowledgeable, loyal, and desirous of freedom for job enhancement, and can develop systems that will improve job outcome and customer satisfaction if given the opportunity.

- **Customers**—Our goal is to meet or exceed customer expectations. We are continually measuring and evaluating internal and external perceptions of our performance. We use customer feedback to improve our processes and services. We will meet customer needs at all levels and seek their input and direction on how we can better serve them.

- **Diversity in the Workplace**—We can realize the full potential of our workforce if we celebrate both our unity of purpose as an organization and uniqueness as individuals. Through the recognition and affirmation of diversity within our workplace, we foster associates' personal growth, strengthen our ability to respond to challenges, and improve service to our customers.

IDENTIFY THE DESIRABLE OUTCOMES THAT RESULT FROM GOVERNMENT ORGANIZATION EFFICIENCY AND EFFECTIVENESS

The sixth step, a vital one, is to identify the desirable outcomes that result from government organization efficiency and effectiveness. In other words, what should occur as a result of the system? For example, a government organization that pays welfare checks should not judge its effectiveness by reaching its goal, or by meeting a quota of paying people on welfare, but rather by what the organization has achieved to return people on welfare to work. If you provide resources to a government organization, you should expect a return on investment, one higher than required by law. When Florida directed their workers' compensation division to work with insurance companies to pay workers compensation claims, workers compensation grew dramatically every year. More and more people were hired in the division every year, because this division was very successful in administering benefits.

Rather than focusing on prevention, the division focused on detection and payments. The program will continue to grow until the lawmakers and leaders in this area fully concentrate, not on goals developed by the Division of Worker Compensation, but on outcomes. The primary focus of the workers compensation program should be to reduce accidents in the workplace. Their emphasis should not be on how many people they pay, but how many workplace accidents they can reduce. That does not mean that they should just stop administering worker compensation claims, but that they should be recognized and rewarded as an agency if they can have a significant impact on the desirable outcomes, which, in this case, is "no accidents," —which, of course, is the mission of another Division.

Transformational leaders clearly define desirable outcomes and design their organization to achieve them. By not focusing on goals and quotas and focusing instead on desired outcomes, frontliners can use their brain power to help achieve them.

The moment of truth for any organization is when a government customer comes in contact with a front-line associate. What a front-liner thinks should be done on behalf of the customer is the most important moment in the life of the organization. If a front-liner thinks that his or her only task is to obtain accurate information from the client in order to meet a quota, then government will be ineffective. On the other hand, if a front-liner knows what the organization wants to achieve on behalf of the customer and values the desired outcome, he or she will work effectively toward that end.

Transformational leaders empower subordinates to work towards achieving desirable outcomes by first clearly defining those outcomes, and second, by allowing them to decide the best way to achieve the desired outcomes by continually improving their processes.

DEVELOP A STRATEGIC PLAN

Strategic planning is the organization's plan for achieving its desired outcomes. An effective strategy clearly outlines what organizational leaders believe is the most effective use of resources, and how these resources should be used to achieve desirable outcomes.

Traditionally, organizations in government develop annual plans that are first presented to the lawmakers for the purposes of garnering resources. Most government plans begin with goals and objectives, followed by a detailed explanation of how their goals and objectives will be achieved. Practically everyone who has ever dealt with lawmakers in an attempt to secure resources knows that the "real" power for planning and budget exists in the legislative staff, and not with the elected legislators. This is one reason why government is so slow to change. Legislative staff believe that they are the customer of the department, rather than the true customers the department serves. Consequently, enormous energy and time is spent by every government agency in the preparation of their annual plan.

In fact, most government administrators agree with the legislative staff and concentrate on obtaining more resources for their department. Many administrators believe that you should define organizational success based on your success with the legislature. For example, university administrators each year attempt to justify their success by the amount of resources their university receives. Therefore, each year administrators describe how effectively they used last year's resources to justify new resources. Growing the division, or in other words, growing government is their objective.

Making the annual trip with open hands to Capitol Hill will be a part of government for a long time. However, lawmakers are gradually understanding that if they are going to continue funding departments, it will depend more on how customers of government are affected than on performance goals. In our opinion, lawmakers in the twenty-first century will expect government leaders to assist them in achieving desirable outcomes. Lawmakers will expect resources to be used wisely, not just to achieve an isolated goal. They will be asking more questions relative to how customers benefited from the resources they expended and how the taxpayers benefited.

Legislative staff members will have to change the way they think about government. Most of them act as though they are on some kind of power trip and know what is best for the customer. What makes matters worse is that most legislative staff are operating on archaic management principles formulated by scientific management. They cannot understand management unless it is divided into silos, each with its own specific goals. Outdated legislative staff philosophies are perhaps the biggest obstacle to effective government. Viewing organizations as part of a larger system seems to be practically impossible for them. In the department where the authors worked, a topnotch legislative staff member was hired to direct a division. We were shocked as we observed how difficult it was for this former member of the legislative staff to administer a program. This person thought that everything had to be negotiated, and that almost every interaction produced a winner and a loser.

This person felt it was the responsibility of subordinates to meet the director's needs. In other words, the director was the customer and the subordinate's job was to meet or exceed the director's expectations. This director was sincere, but did not understand the organization as a system focused on customers and processes, rather than on the personalities of subordinates. For this director, how to control the personality of the subordinate was far more important than customers and processes. Each subordinate learned quickly that the processes and customers were not important, but that "getting along" with the director was a higher priority. Consequently, each subordinate took the position that the best way to survive in the organization was to "kiss up."

If government organizations continue their annual planning and annual trip to Capitol Hill to grow government, the taxpayers are going to continue to revolt. Rather than government becoming effective, we will continue to go from one extreme to another, from ample resources to very few resources. When resources were plentiful, the true customer still did not win, because the agencies viewed the lawmakers, and particularly the legislative staff, as their customers.

When resources are dramatically cut, the true customer still loses. Therefore, government leaders have to "take the bull by the horns" and change the way they manage government organizations. Leaders have to move away from annually setting goals and quotas to long-term strategic planning.

Strategic planning is the organization's plan for achieving its desired outcomes. Strategic plans focus on customers and are directed toward achieving desired outcomes. This is the plan that all associates will follow. It is not a document that has a fancy cover, or one designed to impress lawmakers, but rather one that guides associates in the direction the organization should go.

Strategic plans involve everyone in the organization. The plan is not something that is delegated to the planning department. Strategic plans are constantly changing and are not just done annually. If organizations rely on the typical approach of planning a year in advance and waiting to see what will happen to their plan during the course of the year, administrators will continue to be detectors and not preventors. They can only detect how well the organization has done at the end of the year.

Smart administrators in traditional organizations know they do not want to be embarrassed at the end of the year by not meeting their goals and quotas. Therefore, they regularly criticize subordinates if monthly quotas are not met. In response, front-line associates, even though they are frustrated because they can't fulfill customer needs, deliver what is expected of them in order to keep their jobs.

When we administered a large department of over 7,000 associates, we developed TQM strategic plans at a minimum during each quarter. Every strategic planning session began with desired outcomes, followed by the mission statement, and a restatement of our values. We then conducted an analysis of our organization by discussing the following topics:

1   Strengths

2. Weaknesses

3. Opportunities

4. Threats

This analysis was used to evaluate how well we were doing in accomplishing the prior strategic plan. We made an assumption— that the organization was in constant change and therefore, leadership had to be in tune with what was occurring in the organization on a "real time" basis, rather than through some theoretical perspective. We knew we had to improve daily just to maintain our gains.

After we evaluated what was occurring as a result of our previous strategic plan, we identified issues which needed discussion in order to improve our organization. For example, if training became an issue, we would review specific data regarding training and then develop an action plan to improve training. One issue that seemed to always surface at every meeting was the lack of leadership by government administrators. We were continually revisiting this issue since many government administrators resisted the concept of empowerment. On the other hand, front line associates, when given the opportunity to work in an empowerment organization, gravitated towards that end.

In a later chapter we will discuss many of the specific strategies we employed. It is important here for the reader to understand that strategic planning is an ongoing activity for which everyone is responsible. Empowerment organizations require "hands-on" planning at all levels of the organization. Every administrator and every leader should constantly be developing a strategic plan to achieve desirable outcomes.

Determining what is the best use of organization resource requires leaders who involve everyone in the organization to provide input. The best input is the data collected by people working in processes who are empowered to improve them. Leaders help associates to realize and fulfill strategic plans, that is to do what they actually planned to do. Vision statements, mission statements, values, and desired outcomes strongly influence strategic planning. Strategic planning teams collect and analyze data, adopt a plan, and take action to implement their plan. These strategic planning sessions should occur frequently since government organizations are in continual change.

ALIGN ORGANIZATIONS TO ACHIEVE DESIRABLE OUTCOMES

Government bureaucracies are formal organizations where organizational charts clearly identify the chain of command and span of control. Departments, divisions, bureaus, and units are neatly pieced together. Managers' responsibilities are very specific, and formal authority is clearly outlined. Functions are neatly grouped together, as well as people who do similar work. Furthermore, the span of "people" control is a time-honored tradition.

Government organizations in the twenty-first century will be forced to realign systems if they are to be efficient and effective. Government systems will be aligned so that they can deliver value to customers. Rather than attempting to coordinate activities through organization hierarchies by issuing directives from superiors to subordinates, government leaders will redesign systems so that coordination can be achieved by process improvement teams.

Agencies will be aligned around core processes rather than functions. The goal will be to eliminate unnecessary bureaucracy. Leaders and teams will streamline processes. Consequently, levels of bureaucracy will be removed, and organizational charts will reflect the way work is processed in the organization. Government organizations will change from being "tall," where administrators have a narrow span of control with many levels in the chain of command, to a "flat" organization, where leaders will have a wide span of control with fewer levels of management.

Leaders and associates in realigned organizations will be expected to improve processes and therefore, will be empowered to make decisions. As a consequence, decision making will be much faster, and communication will flow across organization boundaries rather than just up and down.

One way to display a realigned organization is to use the core processes, showing how subprocesses in the system are connected to the core process. For example, the vocational rehabilitation subprocess connects directly to department core processes as follows:

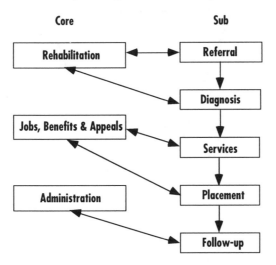

Another way to communicate alignment in the organization is the inverted hierarchy. Most organizations look like a triangle, with the leader at the top, then various levels of management down to the front-line worker, and finally with the customer at the bottom.

If the hierarchy is inverted, the customers appear at the top, front-liners, various levels of management appear next, and finally the leader appears at the bottom.

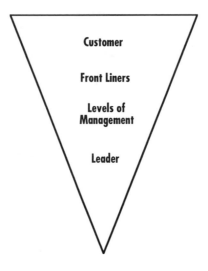

The twenty-first century organization will be much flatter, have fewer levels of administrators, and leaders will have a larger span of control. In an empowerment organization, leaders will not be preoccupied with "people control," but rather focus on "process control."

PRINCIPLES THAT SERVE AS THE FOUNDATION FOR MANAGEMENT ACTION

One final step that is required for transformational leadership is to develop a set of principles that serve as the foundation for management action. These are the principles that every administrator and manager in the organization adheres to and uses to manage in the organization. These principles are interrelated, and all of them are required. In an empowerment organization, one manager cannot use one set of principles while another manager uses a different set of principles.

We believe that the best principles for twenty-first century government organizations have their roots in Total Quality Management. We developed our principles by studying primarily two gurus in the field—W. Edwards Deming and Joseph Juran. We believe that the management methods advocated by Deming and Juran should be applied in government. After all, these Principles were developed by Deming and Juran when they assisted our government during World War II. In 1992, the Department of Labor and Employment Security in Florida allowed us the opportunity to test the Deming and Juran methods. Their ideas became our foundation for developing a management system and principles for government organizations.

As a leader, you might take issue with some of these principles and perhaps can articulate better ones. The important point here is that you select and implement a set of management principles that everyone practices. We believe the following set of principles is effective for government organizations. We tested these principles over a four-year period in the Department of Labor and Employment Security in Florida.

PRINCIPLE #1: Meet or exceed customer expectations.

The goal of an empowerment organization is to meet or exceed customer expectations. Rather than being driven by top managers who interpret what the customer needs and wants, the organization is driven by customer focus. The workers who are assigned a given process are responsible for interpreting customer needs and improving their assigned processes. The vision, the mission, the organizational structure, organizational plan, personnel practices, policies, procedures, and the management system are the responsibilities of top management.

PRINCIPLE #2: Manage the process.

Efficient and effective organizations are achieved by each process within the organization maximizing process capability. To achieve success, organizations should not emphasize the management of functions, nor the management of people, but rather the management of interconnecting processes. The lessons we learned from the management of organizations in the 1960s and 1970s—that a specific function and specific people could be performing well, yet the total organization could not deliver a quality product—should never be forgotten.

A Total Quality Managed organization is only as good as its weakest process. Therefore, each process demands the attention of those personnel assigned to the process, as well as top management.

PRINCIPLE #3: Data collection and analysis is an ongoing activity.

Each associate assigned to a process is responsible for collecting and analyzing data that emerges from the study of each activity, along with inputs, outputs, and outcomes. Each process, for example, will identify the time, errors, and the amount of rework within a process. It is not the measurement of people, but rather the measurement of quality indicators within the process that leads to continual process improvement.

PRINCIPLE #4: Decisions are data-based.

By using continual improvement tools and methods, organizational members generate meaningful data that is used to make decisions that lead to continual process improvement. Data and information are collected from a variety of both internal and external sources. The collection is a systematic effort that provides valid information to be used by employees to analyze and improve the work processes. Decisions reached within teams and by top management are thus based upon valid data rather than "gut-level" feelings.

PRINCIPLE #5: Process improvement requires supplier/customer and organizational partnerships.

In state government, the "suppliers" include our referral agencies, the vendors that supply services, and may include employers, whose former employees are customers now served by the department's processes. Each of these suppliers has a vital interest in the success of the customer's program, and each shares the benefits resulting in quality services.

On the other end of the process are our customers who receive our products. It is critical that we continually measure our customer's needs and expectations through a variety of techniques, including surveys, focus groups, etc.

PRINCIPLE #6: Process improvement teams are responsible for continual improvement.

Teams are assigned the analysis of the process and are empowered to meet the needs of the customer. They honor the quality principles and identify and evaluate potential improvement opportunities. They are empowered to implement suggested changes and to verify results.

PRINCIPLE #7: Organizational communication and recognition are shared responsibilities.

Being open and honest regarding organizational communication is a requirement for a quality-managed organization. No data, whether it be positive or negative, should be withheld from associates. For an organization to be effective, associates must be trusted and respected. Therefore, it should not be the role of upper management to tell associates only what they "need" to know, but rather to share information at all levels. To make improvements, associates must not only understand what is occurring in the process to which they are assigned, but also in all other processes as well.

The role of upper management is to assure associates that no matter what data is generated from their work, as long as the data is accurate, the data will be treated in a positive manner. If top management does not trust its associates, and people are punished for delivering bad news regarding quality indicators, then it will be impossible to drive out fear in the organization. If there is fear in the organization, management is likely to get only data that "fits" their wants and needs. An organization managed by fear frequently generates data that is designed to make management look good, instead of showing customer dissatisfaction or faults within the system.

PRINCIPLE #8: Train all associates.

Traditional management practices assumed that management knew best. Therefore, management's job was to tell the employees what to do and employees" job was to do what they were told. Management training was reserved only for managers. In a empowerment organization, however, everyone is treated with respect, and everyone receives management training since it is everyone's responsibility to work together in managing a process.

PRINCIPLE #9: Process performance is measured by quality indicators, outputs, and out comes. Personnel are recognized and rewarded for their contributions to process improvement, and process performance.

Managing performance in a TQM organization is not a simplistic process. It is not a matter of meeting a quota or a goal. Nor is it a matter of just doing an assigned task. Rather, a worker in an empowering organization fulfills many roles and accepts numerous responsibilities. Workers are expected to take ownership of their assigned processes and are empowered to make continual improvements.

Workers do not work in competition with other workers, but rather work in cooperation. Therefore, they are rewarded for their contributions as individuals and team members. Furthermore, performance assessment includes a variety of instruments, including assessments made by customers, suppliers, team members, and management.

Managers use the same instruments, as well as evaluations by subordinates.

PRINCIPLE #10: Leadership is empowering others to do the right thing the first time, creating a customer orientation, let ting data drive decisions, role modeling quality val- ues, being highly visible and actively involved, and recognizing associates who make continual improve- ments.

Effective leaders must be "out front." They must make it clear that meeting or exceeding customer expectations is the driving force and that associates must look to the customer for direction. It is not the leader's interpretation of what the customer needs and wants, but rather data that is derived from customer analysis which motivates process improvements. Leaders aim at process control, not at controlling people. Leaders manage the process, not people. They set forth the vision, help construct the mission, de- velop a culture so all associates can practice the values, and recognize associates who contribute towards making continual improvements.

Leaders respect people, have high expectations of them, and enable associates to attain quality work and a high level of perfor- mance. Leaders have high energy and energize others.

SUMMARY

In this chapter, we have presented a strategy (course of action) that will guide a transformational leader in implementing em- powering systems. This plan includes the following steps:

- Create a vision for the organization.

- Develop a mission statement.

- Establish organization values.

- Identify the desirable outcomes that result from government organization efficiency and effectiveness.

- Develop a strategic plan.

- Align organizations to achieve desirable outcomes.

- Develop a set of principles that serve as the foundation for management action.

CHAPTER 4

TRANSFORMATIONAL LEADERSHIP: CHARACTERISTICS

For years, the study of leadership focused primarily on trying to identify characteristics frequently associated with leaders. At one point in history, characteristics often associated with effective leadership strongly influenced leadership selection. A characteristic is a distinguishing feature, and in this chapter means to distinguish qualities associated with leadership. To possess a quality means to possess a characteristic that is distinctive or special. For example, at one time in history effective leaders were characterized as being male, authoritarian, masculine, independent, intelligent, creative, and empathetic. They were also characterized as being older, more experienced, generally tall, attentive of their appearance, extroverts, very talkative, ambitious, and dominant.

Many organizations even trained managers so that they would exemplify these characteristics. The obvious problem with making assumptions about the precise characteristics of a leader is that one's assumptions can be wrong. Trying to enhance leadership effectiveness in an organization by selecting only those individuals who "look like leaders," or are masculine and older, is not only invalid, but now illegal.

Being a transformational leader requires much more than exemplifying these characteristics. The purpose of this chapter is to identify those elements that characterize transformational leaders. We are not suggesting that a person having these characteristics will automatically be a transformational leader. We are suggesting, however, that these characteristics are helpful if an individual is attempting to influence others in an empowerment environment. These characteristics do not ensure success, but rather may enhance leadership effectiveness.

Furthermore, a person could have characteristics of transformational leadership but not necessarily always display them. People should not be selected for leadership positions just because they display certain characteristics, but rather an individual should understand that developing these characteristics will enhance their effectiveness.

Transformational leaders cause change; they do not just react to change. They have a vision and mission that requires them to empower others, whereas traditional bureaucratic administrators attempt to garner power for the purpose of protecting themselves, their job, and their followers. It is not unusual to find many government administrators spending much of their time developing a power base with state lawmakers, primarily to protect themselves and their department. Transformational leaders, on the other hand, understand that power is in the system, and if the system delivers desirable outcomes, there will be plenty of accolades for all involved.

Leaders in government should assess themselves to see how they rate relative to the characteristics identified. We believe that transformational leaders should adopt these characteristics because it is difficult to empower people without them. This is not to say that they are mandatory, but they do enable a person not only to be effective, but also to endure the process of empowering others. We have observed many government administrators who make the claim that they want to empower others, but are sadly lacking in these characteristics.

For example, we observed one leader who claimed that she wanted to empower front-liners, but found it very difficult to accept opinions that were contrary to his thinking. Furthermore, he was unwilling to risk front-liners making changes in the system. He needed to be convinced that each change was absolutely necessary and wanted to be certain about each move. Consequently, it was practically impossible for him to become an effective transformational leader.

James M. Kouzes and Barry Z. Posner studied empowerment characteristics and presented them in their book, *The Leadership Challenge*, published by Jossey Bass Publishers, San Francisco, in 1987. After surveying 5,000 managers, including 800 senior executives in the Federal government, they discovered several essential tests that a person must pass before being labeled a leader. They found the top four characteristics of superior leaders to be honest, competent, forward-looking, and inspiring.

The results found by Kouzes and Posner are similar to the top five characteristics selected by AT&T employees, which characterized leaders as honest, competent, inspiring, courageous, and forward-looking.

To these we maintain that the following characteristics enable transformational leaders:

1. High tolerance for uncertainty.

Empowerment of the work force is frequently discussed, but seldom implemented. When the authors were implementing Total Quality Management in the state agencies, we were overwhelmed to find so many government administrators who were uncomfortable with change. It would seem like the work force would be the biggest obstacle to TQM success; however, it was just the opposite— it was the administration. Administrators could more easily find ten reasons not to empower their work force, than to find one reason to do it.

We believe that one of the reasons that so many administrators rejected change was because they couldn't tolerate the uncertainty of change. We began to believe that one of the recurring characteristics of a government administrator was an inability to tolerate uncertainty, and that government attracted administrators with this characteristic. We felt that one of the most significant differences between managers in industry and administrators in government was that administrators in government needed to be more secure in their environment. Fortunately, this belief did not hold true with all government administrators. Once we were able to open the system, leaders at various levels emerged, with some taking a major risk if their superior was adamantly opposed to TQM.

Transformational leaders do not just contend with change, they cause change. They do not contend with uncertainty, but rather create environments of uncertainty. Unfortunately, many administrators would be very happy if the world stopped changing and if they could continue the status quo for the rest of their life.

Leaders in government must come to grips with the fact that uncertainty is part of every leader's job. Lack of information about future events, as well as the unknown, comes with the territory. Leaders have to be understanding and tolerate other viewpoints without necessarily agreeing with or even sympathizing with them. When leaders cause change in an organization, they are never certain what will happen. Leaders are uncertain about various issues everyday, and this should not be an uncomfortable feeling, but rather an exciting experience.

2. Low tolerance for certainty.

In leadership, there is a significant difference between certainty and uncertainty. In our study of leadership, we found that the most effective leaders in government can tolerate uncertainty, but on the other hand, have a low tolerance for certainty.

Certainty means that an issue is settled or determined. For example, when organizations adopt cornerstones, beliefs, a mission, values, and management principles, they do so with a high degree of certainty. Organization leaders believe that the aforementioned ideas are the foundation for managing the organization. They publish and respect cornerstones, beliefs, their mission, their values, and management principles with the conviction and certainty that upholding them leads to organizational effectiveness.

We have found that when such certainty exists, the most effective leaders in the organization have a low tolerance for associates, particularly administrators, who do not abide by them. There is an old saying, "you get what you tolerate." We have observed administrators who, either do not have convictions about leadership and organization principles, or when they do have convictions, are afraid to enforce them.

Many administrators in government constantly complain about lacking resources and good people. They tolerate incompetence, and then complain about it. Transformational leaders are not just "willy nilly wimps." Quite the contrary, transformational leaders have strong convictions, and a low tolerance for people who have been trained to understand and implement their convictions, but for one reason or another choose not to.

We believe that one of the primary reasons that so many administrators have difficulty in becoming transformational leaders is that they do not distinguish between the characteristic of high tolerance for uncertainty, and low tolerance for certainty. Transformational leaders adhere to very strong convictions when they fulfill their responsibility for providing organizational direction and strategy. On the other hand, they have a high tolerance for uncertainty when they are implementing a continual improvement initiative in the organization.

3. Sustained energy.

Energy is the capacity for vigorous action. Being a successful transformational leader requires being an energetic person. In government, the stereotypical administrator is one who comes into the office an hour after everyone else, takes a long lunch, and leaves an hour early. Fortunately, this is not true. Most government administrators work far more hours than are required. Working long hours, however, does not make an administrator a leader. An important characteristic of a transformational leader is the willingness to commit energy to enable and support associates. They are able not only to do their administrative work, but they are able to find time to spend with their associates at all levels. They attend process improvement team meetings and participate as team members. They have energy to carefully review data that is generated by process improvement teams. Rather than hiding in their offices, transformational leaders are constantly on the run, listening to their associates and identifying and removing obstacles that may be impeding team process. They have the energy to teach classes, write articles for the newsletters, and are always ready to give a speech to associates when requested. They find energy to listen and respond to team presentations.

Transformational leaders do not go to work with the intent of sitting in their office, reacting to problems, and having associates come to them. Quite the opposite. They come to work to make a positive contribution. They are energetic.

4. Passion for quality.

Government administrators are rightfully pleased when they achieve goals and quotas. Transformational leaders go far beyond the ordinary. In fact, they are extreme. They have a compelling drive that is so intense that they desire extraordinary results, are intensely enthusiastic, and have a personal goal of surpassing all previous records of performance. For some internal reason, maybe not even known to them, transformational leaders have a passion for doing the right thing the first time.

One of the biggest problems confronting top government leaders is that they frequently deal with elected leaders who have a passion for politics and not necessarily for quality or customer satisfaction. Leaders that have a passion for politics frequently make decisions that benefit political careers, not necessarily government itself. We have been exposed to many politicians who have convinced the public that they are for quality government, but ultimately will make decisions on issues and political appointments that are contrary to their espoused position.

It is often discouraging to observe politicians who vigorously attack government systems and employees while running for election or trying to get media coverage, and yet are not willing to spend any time in government agencies to understand the agency's strategy for efficiency and effectiveness. Many government administrators understand this hypocrisy, and realize that it is to their personal benefit that it continues. In fact, we listened to government administrators criticize us for even suggesting that we involve elected officials in helping our agency to improve.

We had to face a very harsh reality—that many government administrators were willing to accept the status quo, and many elected officials were not interested in helping government become a quality government. Obviously, if government is going to be efficient and effective, it is going to take leaders—political, elected, or appointed—who have the drive, the desire, and the passion to continually improve government processes. It will take leaders who are driven, not by or for the sake of power, but rather by the empowerment of others.

5. Perseverance.

Opposition, obstacles, annoyances, etc. occur daily when you have a passion for quality. What is so intriguing about transformational leadership is that you are trying to give people power to control their processes, and yet you find so much resistance. In our attempts to empower people, it felt like it was a daily tug-of-war. We were pulling for front-liners to manage their assigned processes, and many of them were resisting our attempts. We constantly heard associates complain about how people in the upper levels of government did not understand what they did, did not care much, and when management made a decision, it was the wrong one.

When we attempted to turn the tables and empower them to make decisions, we met resistance at all levels. It was somewhat predictable that upper level administrators would resist the change, since many of them thought the people who worked in government at lower levels were basically lazy and leaned towards being incompetent. Only through tight control could administrators insure that their workers would do what they were told to do. Furthermore, many front-liners resisted any attempts by the organization to change the system, since they resented being controlled and distrusted by administrators.

We were also bewildered at how many government employees resented our attempts to train and develop them. We have always maintained that the time and money an organization invested in workers represented an honor and an opportunity. In today's fast changing work environment, every worker should be afraid of not having the knowledge and skills to compete and of being ineffective at work. Unfortunately, many government workers have the attitude that government is so slow to change that they will be in retirement by the time new skills and knowledge are required. Furthermore, some believe that a job is an assigned task that is not likely to change.

Many, in fact, take the position that government administrators should "just leave them alone," and everything will be fine. These workers are either unaware of the dramatic organizational change that is now occurring in government, or refuse to believe it. They fail to acknowledge that if they do not improve their work processes, there will be someone reinventing how the work can better be done with technology. In other words, if you are not improving your job, someone else is trying to. There is not a competent professional today that is not spending part of each day learning something new just to maintain the gains made in the past.

Transformational leaders understand that all workers in an organization must have a professional attitude. They need each and every person to be knowledgeable and skilled. Therefore, when opposition emerges, when obstacles are thrown in front of them, they do not quit. Rather, transformational leaders accept the challenge. Even when insulted, even when those who work for them criticize them behind their backs, they persevere. Transformational leadership requires that you "respect those who don't respect you." Transformational leaders are tenacious, adhere to their convictions, and are unrelenting in their desire to instill beliefs, values, and principles in others.

6. Positive self-image.

Believing in yourself is a characteristic that enables empowerment. People who are insecure in their personal beliefs about themselves find it very difficult to empower others. They are afraid to empower others because they fear the consequences. If they do not believe in themselves, they often do not believe in others. If they do not feel that their work is meaningful and adds value and if they hold themselves in low esteem, they are unlikely to respect others and empower them.

Transformational leaders need to be mentally tough. Their self-image must be so positive that they can properly and effectively deal with people who vigorously attempt to destroy their concepts. We have observed people who have been appointed to the highest levels in government organizations, who were insecure about their beliefs and had very poor self-images. These highly placed bureaucrats caused nothing but misery for their followers. It appeared that they stood for nothing, were against any change, and spent their time reacting to problems every day. They were afraid of the press, afraid of the legislature, and even afraid of the people who worked for them. They feared negative newspaper articles and even anonymous letters. Every day there was a major tremor in the organization that required them to have a meeting to see what defensive strategy could be employed. Furthermore, they thought their telephones were bugged, their offices were bugged, and there always seemed to be someone to be distrusted.

Transformational leaders have a positive mental picture of themselves. They see themselves as honest, intelligent, knowledgeable about their organization, proactive, and visionary, with a genuine concern for people and their organization. They project this positive self-image to instill empowerment. Having a positive self-image allows them to acknowledge their strengths, as well as weaknesses, and enables them not to fear failure. They perceive themselves as being successful, not failures. Consequently, they are not afraid to put their self-interest second and the interest of the organization first. Their positive self-image allows them to grant empowerment to others for the purpose of process control.

On the other hand, administrators with a low self-image attempt to control the behaviors of others as a way to get others to respect them. In other words, transformational leaders have such a high respect for themselves that they do not need to force others to respect them because of their position. In fact, it is just the opposite. Transformational leaders lose respect for themselves when they do not respect others. They improve their self-images by empowering and supporting others. The more they are successful at empowering others, the more they think of themselves as winners. Many people with a positive self-image believe they are "lucky" because they are excited about all of the good things that happen as a result of their leadership. They know there is not always a direct cause-effect relationship between their leadership and a specific positive action. They attribute the positive action to many causes and therefore believe that they are "lucky."

7. Credibility.

A characteristic that is mandatory for any person who desires to influence others is credibility. Credibility is defined as the perceived trust you attach to a person. It has two dimensions: authoritativeness and character. The first dimension, authoritativeness, is the perception followers have regarding a leader's competence, authority, and reliability. You can measure authoritativeness by answering the following questions:

1. Is the leader informed?

2. Is the leader intelligent?

3. Is the leader qualified?

4. Is the leader reliable?

5. Is the leader valuable to the organization?

Transformational leaders with high credibility will be perceived positively by followers in answering all of the above questions. We have observed leaders who have received favorable ratings on all the questions but one, and still were considered as being a very low credibility source. For example, a highly placed leader was extremely informed and highly qualified and intelligent, but was considered unreliable by his peers and followers. He constantly forgot meetings, his work was often turned in late, and he flippantly responded to suggestions that he might improve his ability to meet his commitments.

The second dimension of credibility, character, is the perceived pattern of behavior that people attach to morality and reputation. To assess the character of a leader, the following questions may be used:

1. Is the leader honest?

2. Is the leader friendly?

3. Is the leader pleasant?

4. Is the leader nice?

5. Is the leader unselfish?

Again, to be judged as a person of high character, you must score highly on all questions. Followers will not ascribe high character to an individual who may be honest, friendly, pleasant, and nice, but who is also selfish. It requires a positive perception by followers on all of these questions to be judged as having high character.

Transformational leaders need to be perceived as having high credibility by most of their followers. Obviously, not every person in the organization is going to ascribe high credibility to a leader. In today's environment, leaders are not often perceived as having high credibility. Furthermore, there are many situations where an individual might be judged as having low credibility, and in another situation be judged as having high credibility. Transformational leaders know that they must maintain high credibility relative to empowerment issues in the organization. In other words, followers must perceive the transformational leader as being reliable, informed, qualified, intelligent, and valuable to the organization regarding their attempt to empower the organization. Furthermore, they must perceive the transformational leader as being honest, friendly, pleasant, nice, and unselfish.

It is important to remember that a transformational leader does not have to have credibility with each individual within the organization. But rather, the leader must be perceived overall as having credibility. Transformational leaders are characterized as authoritative and trustworthy. They live up to their commitments and "do what they say they are going to do." They start meetings on time, return phone calls, and are always available to help and support their associates. They cannot be successful unless they are perceived as having high credibility.

8. Strong desire to influence others.

Having a strong need to influence others does not mean you have a need to control them. Many administrators prefer to exercise their authority and command, regulate, or even restrain behavior. On the other hand, to influence means to affect the actions of other people without the exertion of authority. To influence implies that you affect another based on the strength of your character, expertise, or knowledge. Transformational leaders have a need to control processes, not people. Transformational leaders have a strong need to influence people, to get them to accept the concepts that they advocate. They want their followers to conclude on their own that these concepts are valuable and worthwhile.

Transformational leaders have a strong need to share their concepts and beliefs, not just with people to whom they report or with their peers, but with everyone in the organization. They are willing to endure hostile personal attacks, enjoy conflict if it is perceived as being beneficial, and even engage in a good argument as long as the debate results in continual improvement. They relish the opportunity to convince another person that their concepts are logical.

We have observed a number of administrators in government leave a meeting that they thought was ineffective or not worthwhile. Rather than trying to influence the outcome of the meeting, the administrator goes behind closed doors to complain about the meeting to people who can be trusted.

Transformational leaders may leave a meeting not satisfied with the results, but it will not be because they did not do whatever they could to influence others to accept another point of view. Many government meetings seem to include everyone, and many in attendance are mere parasites. These people are there just to listen, watch, and then complain. This does not mean that transformational leaders dominate meetings and have to do all the talking. Transformational leaders find it very appropriate to not say anything as long as the meeting is progressing effectively and contributing toward continual improvement.

The authors vividly remember a leader who attended a three-hour meeting and hardly said a word. When we asked him after the meeting why he was so quiet, he stated, "there was no need for me to comment since we were progressing so well." He understood since he was the highest ranking person in the room, his influence was felt. Furthermore, he recognized that when you empower people, other transformational leaders will emerge. It does not take rank and position to be a transformational leader. It does take, however, a strong desire to influence others.

SUMMARY

Transformational leaders have a high tolerance for uncertainty, and as described, a low tolerance for certainty. They are energetic and have a passion for quality. Perseverance is a key ingredient given the many individuals who resist change. In addition, transformational leaders must have a positive self-image, be credible to all, and finally, have a strong desire to influence others.

CHAPTER 5

THE SKILLS OF
TRANSFORMATIONAL LEADERS

A skill is an ability to perform a sequence of behaviors that relates to a specific outcome. For example, some people have the ability to convince others that they are correct, i.e., skills of persuasion. Such people can sequence their behavior to attain a performance goal. In other words, they can convince another person that it is in their best interest to agree with them.

Effective government administrators usually have developed the following skills: they are diplomatic, tactful, knowledgeable, organized, conceptual, persuasive, creative, and social. They usually lean towards the traditional view of leadership, where they see their job as using their power to direct, drive, and control followers. These administrators generally focus on the task at hand, and often ignore personal relationships whenever possible. They often seek opinions from subordinates, but never relinquish the power to make final decisions. They maintain control of group meetings, preventing disruptive behavior and irrelevant discussions. They often discourage subordinates from expressing their true feelings. They are more interested in a rational discussion without emotional outbursts. Finally, they are often preoccupied with establishing their authority and will react negatively to anyone who threatens their authority.

Traditional administrators who take this view of leadership tend to develop leadership skills that lead them towards increasing their power and improving their ability to direct and control their followers. They are likely to attend leadership skill courses that cover such topics as assertiveness, conflict resolution, motivation, decision making, planning, communication, control, and stress management.

Traditional approaches to leadership assume that wisdom and skills of the leader are the most important variables to effectiveness. For example, traditional approaches to leadership argue that leaders need to be creative, and therefore, need to develop their creativity skills. While transformational leaders recognize that personal creativity is an asset, they know their most creative assets are their people. While transformational leaders recognize that their personal decision-making skills are important, they go one step further. They know that effective decision making can best be achieved by people. While transformational leaders recognize that it is an asset to have conflict resolution skills, they believe it is far more effective to empower people in teams to solve their own conflicts. To be an effective transformational leader, it is important that you have a positive self-image. However, it is just as important that you have the skills to enable others to have a positive self-image.

It is vital that transformational leaders recognize that they do not learn new skills just to separate themselves from their followers. In fact, it is just the opposite. Transformational leaders improve their skills with the intent of improving others. The excitement of being a transformational leader comes from observing the improvement in the people they lead. The purpose of this chapter is to identify transformational leadership skills which result in the personal improvement in others. Empowerment energizes one's ability to make an effective presentation, and more important, creates a marvelous feeling when one observes a follower make an effective presentation.

To be a skillful transformational leader, it is helpful to have the traditional leadership skills to be creative, able to communicate effectively, organized, persuasive, and social. However, these skills are insufficient. A transformational leader needs far greater skills since the goal is to develop these skills in others. Transformational leaders do not perceive themselves as all knowledgeable or the final authority on all subjects, but rather as facilitators, teachers, and team builders. They regard themselves highly as a personal asset to the organization, but they know that their success, and the success of their organization, is dependent upon their number one asset, the people who work in the organization.

For years, we have heard traditional administrators talk about people being their "number one" asset, while they in fact ignore them. On the other hand, transformational leaders know that it is in the best interest of government to unleash the potential of its work force. Therefore, transformational leaders create an environment that is conducive for people to use their talents to continually improve the organization.

Granting the authority to others to act on behalf of the organization requires multiple skills. On occasion, cynics of empowerment initiatives suggest that, "since they are going to turn the zoo over to the animals," there is nothing for them to do as an administrator. Nothing could be further from the truth. In fact, transformational leaders have to be extremely skillful. Traditional government administrators frequently attempt to develop their skills in the art of delegation. They concentrate on delegating some of their power to subordinates in order to get the job done. Effective delegation requires that precise directions be given to the subordinate and be acted upon according to instructions.

Empowerment skills are far more complex, since they enable subordinates to make decisions and take actions that are not prescribed. Instead, subordinates are allowed to make decisions that they believe are in the best interest of improving the process to which they are assigned. In other words, subordinates are granted the power to make decisions and take actions that improve the process without leaders telling them what to do and how to do it. Transformational leadership requires new skills that fall into three categories: conceptual, technical, and communication.

CONCEPTUAL SKILLS

Government organizations are often very complex, and sometimes relationships are ambiguous. Effective transformational leaders must have the skills to conceptualize relationships and have the ability to see the "whole" organization. Much of their day is spent in conceptualizing how various parts of the organization relate to each other, and how a change in one part of the organization affects the entire organization. Furthermore, transformational leaders excel at forming concepts when new information becomes available. They are often able to develop new ideas and add new meaning to a situation. They are able to review information and discover new ways to improve their processes, or find another way to communicate to subordinates. By possessing strong conceptual skills, transformational leaders are able to be proactive, to initiate activities, and to prevent problems, rather than waiting for a problem to develop before reacting to it. Furthermore, when confronted with the problem, they have the skill to review a broad range of information and formulate multiple alternatives.

To develop and exercise conceptual leadership skills, we suggest the following three activities:

1. Monitor your environment.

2. Understand your organization's processes.

3. Continually employ strategic planning.

---

1. Monitor your environment.

Many government administrators think only about the job at hand. They are concerned about not making a mistake, embarrassing their boss, or not meeting their quotas. Sometimes it is very difficult for them to "think out of their box."

Transformational leaders, on the other hand, are able to conceive their job in a broader framework. They constantly monitor their internal as well as their external environment. They are not only concerned about what is occurring in their state capitol or in

Congress, but are also in tune with the most recent developments internally and externally. Internally, they are constantly observing what is happening in their organization, and are interacting with their staff and other members of the organization for the purpose of diagnosing conditions in their organization. They are evaluating the effects of organization policies, procedures, decision making, and strategy. Outside of their organizational boundaries, they continually monitor the effects of their organization on their customers, on their suppliers, and on taxpayers. They also monitor the developments occurring in other government as well as business organizations. By monitoring internal and external environments, transformational leaders significantly increase their skill in conceptualizing strategies that lead to improving their organization.

2. Understand organization processes.

Traditional administrators frequently see the organization in boxes. Rather than seeing how the work is actually processed, they conceive of the organization as reflected by the organizational chart. It is difficult to use your conceptual skills if you are "boxed" in. Therefore, transformational leaders conceive of the organization as a system that transforms inputs to outputs and ultimately, outcomes. To effectively use your conceptual skills, you need to understand how work flows in your organization. Therefore, we recommend that you flowchart your organization's work flow and conceive of your organization not as having specific functions, but as a complete process. Transformational leaders are "process thinkers." They understand that they can more effectively use their conceptual skills if they think in terms of processes, and not functions. Furthermore, when processes are viewed as a complete system in a flowchart, it is possible to expand horizons and conceive new frameworks, new ideas, or hypotheses.

A flowchart is a graphic representation of the flow of work. It is a map of what occurs. The flowchart shows the what order work is performed in, what takes place, and even who is doing it at times. It is a common reference that all team members can examine to understand the process. It is a picture that all can agree upon and that can be shared with others not on the team. The flowchart is an outstanding tool to share with new associates just joining the organization, for they can then readily see what actually takes place in a process.

When you have completed your flowchart you will be able to examine the process to ask the following questions:

- Are there any "loops" in the process? Why?

- Does each step add value? Could a step be eliminated?

- Where are the delays? Why?

- Where are measurements taken? Why?

3. Continually employ strategic planning.

Strategic planning is required for achieving the organization's mission. It details how organization resources are deployed. Government administrators are frequently conditioned by the annual strategic plan. In the year prior to the implementation of a plan, top echelon managers provide data to the planning unit, whose primary goal is to prepare a plan which is sent to the legislative and executive branches of government for approval. If approved, the plan is implemented the following year.

Provided this is the case, conceptual skills are only required annually. Once the plan is conceived and approved, then administrators are assigned the task of implementing it. In reality, however, government organizations are far more complex; therefore, conceptual skills need to be developed and exercised continually. We found that weekly strategic planning sessions were extremely valuable when we were responsible for a large department in the Florida state government. These sessions assisted government leaders in not only developing conceptual skills, but also created new responses to old problems and generated ideas for new opportunities. Our strategic planning sessions used the following agenda:

1. Review mission

2. Review values

3. Identify organizational strengths

4. Identify organizational weaknesses

5. Identify opportunities

6. Identify threats

7. Develop action plan

TECHNICAL SKILLS

Traditional administrators in government frequently think of technical skills as being related to technology or specific knowledge about technical matters regarding the law or procedures. Transformational leaders understand that this perception of technical skills is inadequate. They realize that if they are to empower others, they need to expand their skills so that they can not only comprehend the effects of organizational processes, but also to add value to process improvement. Merely using technology and following procedures is insufficient. Transformational leaders must not only understand how to use technology and follow procedures, but also how to effectively use technical skills in measuring and improving processes.

Transformational leaders use their technical skills to set priorities and evaluate process effectiveness. Obtaining meaningful and accurate data, along with statistical competence, is a skill that will help leaders to avoid overreacting to incidents, and to respond in a controlled, strategic manner. Transformational leaders are skilled in using the following fundamental quality tools:

HISTOGRAMS

The Histogram is like a picture of a lot of data. The picture shows the variation in data that would be difficult to interpret if all one had was a set of numbers. Almost everything we measure can have variation. For example, if we were to measure the time it takes for a customer to see an interviewer in a state agency, we would probably see a great deal of variation. Perhaps, if the customer is fortunate, she will be seen in 15 minutes, while another might have to wait 35 minutes. The waiting time varies, perhaps dependent upon when the customer arrives at the office.

The histogram helps display this variance in data in a scientific way so that it is easier to see variations, patterns, etc. If a second histogram is developed with data taken at a different office, or perhaps on a different day, a comparison of the two histograms might be useful to a team as they address improvements in the process.

A histogram may look like a simple bar chart, but it contains more information. In fact, the creation of the histogram is credited to a Frenchman, A. M. Guerry, who was interested in showing how crime was affected by the age of the criminal. Rather than merely showing the number of crimes in a bar chart, Guerry went a step further and showed how crime was influenced by the age of the criminal through the use of a histogram. His charts clearly showed the number of crimes by age category, something that had not been done previously.

A histogram is actually a bar chart of a frequency distribution of a continuous variable. Examples of continuous variables include time, length, age, count, etc. The histogram shows the relative frequency of occurrence of the data being examined, displays the distribution of the data, and demonstrates the extent to which the data approximates the expected type of curve.

CAUSE AND EFFECT DIAGRAMS

The Cause and Effect Diagram, also known as the "fish-bone" diagram, can be used to identify all potential causes of a given problem. The diagram represents the relationship between an effect (problem) and its potential causes. It is used when you need to identify, explore, and display all of the possible causes of a specific problem or condition. The team first "brainstorms" all possible causes, often spends time between meetings to uncover other reasons for the problem, and then constructs the diagram. Additional brainstorming sessions may be used to minimize the chance of overlooking one or more causes. Most problems have multiple causes, sometimes interacting with each other. Although brainstorming helps identify these causes, the cause and effect diagram displays the causes and shows the interaction that may be occurring.

FORCE FIELD ANALYSIS

One very helpful technique that teams have used may be found in Force Field Analysis. This technique is described in a variety of ways in the literature, but essentially consists of a method of graphically depicting the "forces" working for and against implementation of a new project or process. It is a way to address the concerns often raised by team members that their deliberations and hard work will likely be in vain because "nothing will ever change."

Force field analysis identifies all the various positive and negative forces that will either encourage or discourage change. These forces are displayed and plans can be made to strengthen the positive and eliminate the negative forces. The technique is not just a listing of the forces, but adds a value to each, dependent upon the perceived strength of the factor. For example, a "lack of resources" might receive a weight of 4, vs. "need for training," which might be a 2. In other words, the lack of resources is perceived by the team as far more critical to the success of the new idea or project than the lack of trained staff.

Force field analysis can help move a team along in its deliberations. With its use, the team has identified and recognized the presence of factors that will shape their success. There are often difficult times in a team's work when it is easy to become discouraged if members think that the process improvement stands little chance for acceptance or implementation. Knowing up front that management resistance may be a factor and planning how the team will overcome that factor later, can help team members concentrate on the task at hand.

PARETO CHARTS

The Pareto Chart is a bar chart that clarifies the "important" from the "not-so-important" when examining data. The bars appear in rank order, with the bar on the left showing the greatest number of observations, and the bar on the far right showing the least. A curved line across the top of the graph shows the cumulative percentages so that it is relatively easy to see what factors contribute to, say, 45 percent, 75 percent, or 90 percent of the problem under study.

The Pareto chart is fairly easy to construct and because of its value, is one of the most popular tools used by quality teams. The Pareto chart helps the team concentrate on those factors that are most important. It is relatively easy to be overcome by a multitude of causes and waste time looking at minor issues when working on a problem.

CHECK SHEETS

A Check Sheet is a simple tool designed to make certain that the data is collected and analyzed in a standard way. The check sheet provides order to the collection of data. With this order it is easier for all members of the team to understand what has been collected and what conclusions might be made from an analysis of the data.

The primary uses for the check sheet, in addition to providing organization to collected data, are to help the team begin to find patterns in the data and to begin finding areas where problems may be concentrated. The major task in using a check sheet, other than collecting the data, is the decision of what data will be displayed and the how the sheet will be designed. Therefore, before designing the check sheet and collecting the data, the team will have to decide what they consider important and what they wish to measure. The team may refer to the flowchart they have developed for the process under consideration, or may examine their cause and effect diagram to see where data may be collected.

CONTROL CHARTS

The Control Chart is a Run Chart that makes use of statistical formulas to define Upper Control Limits (UCL) and Lower Control Limits (LCL). The control chart identifies when a process is out of control, so that the cause(s) can be analyzed. When the process is in control, no effort is made to adjust the process. The UCL and LCL are determined by examining the results of the process by taking samples and using a series of statistical formulas. The goal of the control chart is a simple one—to signal when a process is in or out of control. Even the best processes will not produce 100 percent "ideal" results. You can count on some variability present in anything. If the process is in control, however, the variances will fall within the control limits. Outcomes will vary without setting a trend or a cycle of any kind. The reasons for these variances are small and numerous, but of no concern, because they fall within the control limits. One way to influence these minor variances would be to change the system with a new process.

RUN CHARTS

Sometimes called a Trend Chart, the Run Chart helps track data over a specific time period and enables the team to spot patterns or trends. This chart can also be used to spot unusual events or to continuously monitor performance. Run charts are very common and appear in daily publications. You may be familiar with the run charts found in newspaper financial pages showing the rise and fall of the stock market.

A central line in the chart provides the mean or average. The primary use for the Run Chart, by a quality improvement team, would be to understand what is happening in the process under study. For example, if waiting time in lines is under study, a run chart listing the average times in a line at various times during the day would provide data on when customers are likely to come in for services. The chart will show increasing or decreasing trends, and may assist the team in potential process changes.

SCATTER DIAGRAMS

The Scatter Diagram is a tool that is used to display the effects of one variable on another to determine the possible relationships between the variables. It is a graphic representation between two variables. Through this graphic display is it possible "to see" if any relationship exists. Be warned, however, that just because the relationship appears, there is no guarantee that one variable causes the other. A classic example of this may be seen in the current debate concerning violence on television and our increasing crime rate. Both have increased in the past ten years; however, seeing violence on television may not cause it in the streets. There may well be a number of other factors contributing to the increase in crime. We have also seen an increase in the number of cellular telephones during this same time period, and if we used a scatter diagram to plot these two trends, we might be tempted to say that crime caused the increase in cellular telephone use. It is appropriate to use a scatter diagram when the team is questioning the "cause-effect" relationship between two variables and wishes to display this relationship.

COMMUNICATION SKILLS

Communication is a process where a message sender intentionally stimulates a desired message in the mind of a receiver. Sometimes the speaker's purpose is to inform, to entertain, to persuade, or is a combination of all three. Understanding from the outset that the intent is to persuade, the communicator will entertain and inform while influencing the receiver to select a specific course of action. Traditional administrators always understood the importance of communication skills. To be successful, they sent messages that clearly outlined what they wanted and how it should be done. They practiced their communication skills daily by sending messages upward, downward, and horizontally in the organization. Administrators generally transmitted information upward in the organization relating to job assignment, performance, problems, organizational practices or policies, and the methodology for accomplishing tasks. They understood that positive upward communication was more likely to be used by those above them than negative communication. They further understood that upward communication should be timely and was more likely to be accepted if supportive of current policy. They understood that upward communication was more likely to be effective if it went directly to a receiver who could act on it.

On the other hand, downward communication usually dealt with job instructions, rationale, information, and feedback. Although traditional government administrators often understood the importance of horizontal communication, it is often ineffective in traditional government organizations. Horizontal communication allows coordination between departments to maximize productivity. It allows problem solving at the level of origin, and thus increases morale and confidence of the individuals involved in the problem solving process. It allows sharing of information and is useful in solving intradepartmental and interdepartmental conflict. Finally, it serves as a substitute for upward and downward communications in some situations.

Traditional administrators tend to focus only on the development of interpersonal skills since most of their communication occurs in interpersonal settings, whether they are communicating upward, downward, or horizontally in the organization. From time to time, they may have to manage a meeting that includes only their subordinates or make a presentation to upper management. Consequently, traditional administrators understand that they can improve their communication skills by being knowledgeable about human behavior and are sensitive to the feelings and attitudes of others. Effective administrators are adept at establishing effective relationships and gain cooperation by practicing diplomacy.

Transformational leaders exhibit strong interpersonal skills, however. They realize that if they are going to be effective at empowering others, they must be skillful in communicating in a multitude of settings. Nearly everything associated with empowerment systems has to do with facilitating effective communication. Although transformational leaders spend some of their time sending messages to convince upper management, their peers, and their subordinates that they have the solution to a problem, most of their time is spent using their communication skills to facilitate change and to solve problems. Rather than looking to themselves for all of the answers to problems in the organization, they look to others for answers. Therefore, transformational leaders must develop a wide range of communication skills. At a minimum, transformational leaders should develop interpersonal skills, as well as communication skills that empower people and teams. Transformational leaders participate in, facilitate, and lead teams. Furthermore, they must be adept at developing people. Therefore, transformational leaders should acquire communication skills in the following areas: team participation; brainstorming; nominal group technique; team facilitation; team leadership; public speaking; writing , teaching, and coaching.

TEAM PARTICIPATION

Transformational leaders participate in a number of teams. For example, leaders in a government agency might be members of the budget team, strategic planning team, legislative team, etc. Though they may be the highest ranking people in the organization, they need not be a team leader. However, they are expected to be effective participants.

The most effective process improvement team members are people who enjoy working with other people. They value the ideas of others and care about the workplace. They have an intense desire to make improvements in the process and are interested in making decisions that benefit the process. They are comfortable with conflict, put the process first, and realize discussions about membership personalities are not productive. They are forgiving and realize that conflicts will emerge in process improvement.

They do not carry a grudge against another person, but realize that conflict may emerge from differences about what the team should do regarding a recommended action. Effective process improvement team members value personal growth and the personal growth of others. They realize that sharing their views and participating in decision making adds value to themselves and to the process. They appreciate the power of being a team member and enjoy participating on a team, as opposed to trying to solve process problems on their own.

Team members must do all they can to help the team make progress. It is not only the team leader's responsibility to promote effective discussion of issues, but rather each team member shares in this responsibility. Transformational leaders understand and use other team tools that facilitate the team's progress, including those listed below.

BRAINSTORMING

Brainstorming is a way of identifying problems or of generating a number of possible solutions to a problem. It stresses the use of an "open-minded" or "free thinking" approach without criticism of any idea expressed. The goal of brainstorming is to come up with as many ideas as possible without regard to "quality," with as many team members as possible contributing their thoughts. The central concept of brainstorming is to generate a great number of possible ideas, with the agreement by all members that no criticisms be expressed. The quantity of ideas is far more important than the quality of ideas.

The best way to identify the source of problems is to consider all possible causes. In the same manner, the best way to solve problems is to consider all possible solutions. The word "all" is used loosely here, because it is unlikely that any team will ever list every conceivable cause for or solution to a problem. Nevertheless, brainstorming does ensure that people do begin their problem solving with an open mind and not focus on the "obvious" or "usual" causes for, or answers to a problem. Often the obvious or usual ones are not the best.

NOMINAL GROUP TECHNIQUE

The technique know as Nominal Group, or NGT, is one that builds on the brainstorming idea and represents a highly structured approach to generating ideas. NGT is a way to help a small group or team of people survey and clarify their thoughts concerning an issue. Furthermore, the nominal group technique helps the team place in rank order the list of concerns, opinions, or possible ideas to study. It is often used to select a process to study for an improvement effort because an end result of NGT is consensus by team members as to what they consider important. Support to address the process is thus assured. Note that this form of selection, of a process to study, differs from suggestions from management or customers and may not have as much data readily available. The word "nominal" is used in its name because NGT involves nominal discussion vs. open, unregulated discussion in other brainstorming techniques.

Multivoting is another similar technique; however, differs from NGT in one important way. Multivoting involves taking multiple votes by a team to rank or narrow a list of concerns, opinions, or possible areas to study. The process of multivoting is done as a group, whereas NGT involves private decision-making with restricted interaction by group members.

The nominal group technique is an excellent way to produce a wealth of ideas very rapidly. NGT places its focus on the identification and ranking of concerns, opinions, or possible ideas to study, and opens communication by insuring that all members participate. Everyone has an opportunity to contribute and actually is forced to contribute and rank.

TEAM FACILITATION

Transformational leaders are skilled at facilitating team meetings, customer focus groups, customer/organization member meetings, strategic planning sessions, etc. The primary purpose of a facilitator is to guide and to keep individuals on target without having the responsibility of recommending change (or living with the consequences). It is not unusual for team members to "get off the track" in heated discussions. The facilitator intervenes when necessary to bring the team back into focus on its target. Facilitators clarify issues and keep communication flowing freely. They remove obstacles that impede progress. The facilitator insures participation by all members.

On occasion, a team may find that one or two members dominate the discussion. The facilitator brings the less aggressive members into the discussion in a tactful manner. Facilitators support the team, provide motivation, and from time to time, provide the team with training. While all content issues are left to the team, managing conflicts and disruptions, paraphrasing, or interpreting ideas and views, and posing questions to obtain consensus are all considered within the role of the facilitator.

The facilitator uses open-ended questions, ones that cannot be answered with "yes" or "no." They are designed to stimulate thinking and to encourage interaction. Open-ended questions usually begin with "how," "what," and "why." Examples of open-ended questions are:

1. How do you feel about the subject?

2. What is your opinion?

3. Why do you believe this condition exists?

Closed-ended questions are answered with "yes" or "no," or require a short response. They are used to clarify issues. Examples of closed-ended questions are:

1. Do you believe we have covered the subject?

2. How many customers were processed last week?

Team feedback questions are used to seek understanding of issues. For example:

- "Tell me if I heard you correctly," and then paraphrase what was said.

- "I am going to summarize what I believe to be the team's opinion regarding this issue. Tell me if I am accurate."

Team members will frequently ask the facilitator for his or her opinion. Since the facilitator wants to remain neutral, he or she will frequently redirect the question back to the team. For example, if a team member asks the facilitator to resolve a conflict between two team members, the facilitator will take the team member's question and direct it to the entire team.

A team member may ask the facilitator to determine whether another member is right on an issue. In this case, the facilitator would ask the team, "How do you feel about whether the team member is right?" on the issue.

TEAM LEADERSHIP

Leading effective teams is a skill required of transformational leaders. The team leader meets with the team regularly and is responsible for the creation of a good team climate, keeping the team on track, encouraging participation, seeing that ideas are accurately recorded, keeping the meeting positive, and insuring that all ideas are vocalized and respected. The team leader should have a prepared agenda for the initial meeting similar to the one that follows:

1. Welcome.

2. Introduction of team sponsor.

3. Self-introduction by team members.

4. Discuss mission presented by the team sponsor.

5. Discuss roles of members, sponsor, leader and facilitator.

6. Discuss training strategy for participants.

7. Construct series of questions participants would like to have answered.

8. With the team sponsor present, answer questions.

9. Decide on meeting times, dates.

10. Oral evaluation of meeting.

The leader's role is to be out front, enthusiastic, and excited about the prospect of working with this team. During initial meetings, the primary leadership strategy should be one of consideration for all participants. When teams meet for the first time, it can be very stressful for some team participants. People in organizations today are often not comfortable working with teams. There is a lack of trust, and people are afraid that they are going to say the wrong thing. They fear that participation on a team could have a damaging effect on their career.

An important role of the team leader is to create trust and openness. It often takes numerous meetings to overcome resistance of team participants. Therefore, another important trait of the team leader, particularly in the early phases of team development, is patience and consideration. Respect and trust are earned, and the only way the leader can earn them is to demonstrate trust and honesty over time.

PUBLIC SPEAKING

Frequently transformational leaders are asked to formally address audiences composed of associates, especially at awards and recognition ceremonies. They are also often called upon to informally address audiences when they visit team meetings and other organizational meetings. Being an effective speaker is truly an asset for a transformational leader. To develop and practice this skill, we have suggested the following steps to team members preparing to appear before a Quality Council to help them overcome their fears. They can be adopted by anyone preparing a speech or making a presentation before a group.

Guidelines for a Presentation or Speech

1. Remember that people want you to succeed. They do not want you to fail. Everyone has probably faced a similar "ordeal" in their lifetime and would rather enjoy your speech instead of watching you "die" in discomfort. They have empathy for you. They also know the fear of making presentations and most likely will do their best to help you succeed. They are definitely "on your side."

2. Try not to read your presentation or speech. It is far better to use limited key words on a three-by-five card which can be checked periodically. Speak as if you're telling a story to a group of your friends.

3. Celebrate your nervousness. This is a sign that you really care about doing a good job. If you did not care, you would not feel nervous and apprehensive. Everyone who wants to do a good job is nervous. No good actor, comedian, or officer in an association ever appears before a group without feeling nervous. They *all* feel some degree of fear. Nervousness is actually very good if we know how to channel it to our advantage. Stress can be somewhat helpful, if we recognize it and use it effectively.

    Here are some suggestions to help you deal with the stress of public speaking:

    a. Recognize the stress and learn to appreciate it. It is a signal that something great is about to happen. There is little chance that your life will be boring for the next few minutes. Know that this good feeling (the stress) will probably pass in a few minutes, once you are into your presentation.

    b. Play a mental and physical game just before you know you will be on. If possible, take a brisk walk to "charge-up." Walking will loosen you up and will burn off a little energy. Your knees will be in better shape and less likely to shake. Tell yourself that you are the luckiest person in the world at that moment. You get to have people actually listen to you with their full attention. You will not have the usual interruptions in normal conversation. The stage is yours. The very best speakers all "warm up" with similar techniques. They get their juices flowing!

c. If you find that you cannot get up to take a walk, do something else. Actually it is a rare occurrence that you will not have a few moments to walk before your presentation. If you find yourself sitting for thirty minutes just prior to your presentation, do the following:

- Do not sit with your legs crossed. It might just be your luck that one of them will "fall asleep," and you will have difficulty walking when you are called. Wiggle your toes and let your arms drop naturally. Gently twirl your wrists a little to keep the circulation going.

- Check your jaw. Does it feel tense? Loosen it up a bit by wiggling it gently.

- Take a few deep breaths.

4. Give yourself a pep talk. Just before you are scheduled to "go on," take a few minutes to give yourself a positive image.

5. Try not to worry about your hands. Try not to fold them across your chest. It may appear that you are being defensive. Some speakers merely let them hang naturally at their sides. If you feel like you must hold on to something, just touch your thumb to your forefinger on each hand. No one will notice this little touch, but you will know that you are still alive and warm.

6. Move around. If you stand still for long in one place, the audience may think that you have died with your feet planted on the floor.

7. Show your enthusiasm and intensity. Who else in the room can be more enthusiastic or intense about your subject?

8. KISS. In other words, Keep It Short, Stupid. Even though you may be having a grand time and the audience is really giving you good feedback, respect the time allotted. When things are going well, it is too easy to overextend your presentation.

9. Use overhead transparencies that the audience can read and practice using the overhead. If you are going to use an overhead projector, be certain that your overhead transparencies have minimal information per sheet. Do not copy an entire page of typewritten narrative or a table of data that cannot easily be read from the back of the room. Such a transparency is an insult to the audience. Better to present three or four words or statistics per transparency and use more transparencies. Practice and note now the transparency should be placed on the projector so that you are not flipping it over or turning it around needlessly.

10. Get Feedback. Knowing how the audience is perceiving your remarks is critical. How do you do this? Watch their eyes. Their eyes will tell you if they are following along, whether they are questioning your remarks, or if they are lost.

11. Save handouts to the end. If you pass out any material prior to the end of your presentation, you will lose part of your audience. They will be reading. Then you will not be able to see their eyes, will not get any feedback, and will not be certain they heard you. They cannot read and listen at the same time.

WRITING SKILLS

Transformational leaders are often called upon to write an article for the newsletter, clarify policies, write memorandum that are widely distributed, write reports, recognize others with a formal written statement, etc. Being an effective writer enhances leadership effectiveness.

As with oral communication, when writing, your primary consideration is your audience. You need to take into consideration their educational background, culture, motivation, experience, age, etc. Frequently, transformational leaders are trying to make a statement and therefore, are always concerned with the impact of their message. Effective writing is clear and concise. The overall concern is the residual message, what is left over after they have completed reading your document. Therefore, we suggest that you start every written document by understanding your intent and identifying the message or messages you want to leave with your reader. Second, you want to develop an outline of the key points you want to make. Once you have your ideas organized, consider what the reader needs to understand regarding each of your key ideas. We suggest that you use an expressive style where you use the active voice whenever possible. Use action verbs and if possible, write shorter sentences and paragraphs. When you have completed your document, check your grammar, spelling, punctuation, and sentence structure. It is always best to have another person review important documents prior to sending them. Check to see if your residual message comes through as you intended. Check to see if you have provided all the information that is needed. Furthermore, make sure that your document is accurate and that all details are communicated.

Invest in a few good books on writing skills. You are never too old or too skilled to improve your writing.

TEACHING SKILLS

Transformational leaders spend considerable time developing people. A well-educated and trained work force is the most powerful asset for government organizations. Transformational leaders must be skilled in the development of people. They are always looking for opportunities to teach, not just in a formal classroom setting, but also in day to day activities. They find it exciting when they can help an associate look at a concept differently, learn a new skill, or improve his or her self-image. Effective empowerment teachers attain gratification when they can help their associates focus on customers, gather and analyze data, make decisions, flowchart processes and work effectively in teams.

Effective teachers do the following:

1. Involve students.

2. Plan their presentations and discussions. They do not "wing it."

3. Begin and end their discussions or classes on time.

4. Take charge. The participants expect a teacher to be the expert and provide direction.

5. Are friendly and responsive.

6. Challenge participants with clear standards for quality work.

7. Listen to suggestions and incorporate those that are logical and possible.

8. Keep the presentation moving with an occasional change in pace to lower the possibility of monotony. Enthusiasm helps.

9. Respect and praise the participants.

COACHING SKILLS

Transformational leaders spend considerable time developing others. They assist others by providing thoughtful suggestions on what a person or a team can do to improve themselves or situations. They coach their associates. They listen carefully to their associates to identify problems and opportunities that exist for their associates. They help their associates identify personal and organizational goals. They work with their associates to create an action plan for achieving these goals. Along with the associates, they identify actions the associates can take to improve themselves. They are constantly monitoring associates' behavior and, from time to time, make suggestions on how associates might make changes in their behavior or attitude.

An effective coach knows what their associates desire to achieve, takes a sincere interest in helping them to achieve their goals, and is willing to provide feedback regularly on how associates are performing. They are constantly providing reinforcement and constructive criticism. They suggest reading materials and encourage associates to develop their mental skills. They share what they have learned with others. Furthermore, transformational leaders are constantly on the lookout for opportunities that can assist associates in their development. They encourage associates to facilitate meetings, become team leaders, give speeches, write articles, and increase their exposure throughout the organization.

SUMMARY

Transformational leadership requires far more skills than traditional leadership. Such leaders must not only understand how to use the latest technology, but must also learn how to use technical skills effectively in measuring and improving processes. Discussed in the chapter were the fundamental quality tools used by transformational leaders including the histogram, cause and effect diagram, Pareto chart, run chart, scatter diagram, and control chart. Other important communication skills, including public speaking, teaching, writing, and coaching, were shown to be important for successful transformational leaders.

CHAPTER 6

TRANSFORMATIONAL LEADERSHIP BEHAVIOR

---

*"Merit rating rewards people that do well in the system.
It does not reward attempts to improve the system."*

—W. Edwards Deming, *Out of the Crisis*

Having the characteristics and skills of a transformational leader provides the foundation for success. However, the real challenge is to successfully implement these assets in an organization that is designed and developed to use the brain power of associates to continually improve organization processes. Implementing transformational leadership requires behavior that is purposeful and goal directed. The purpose of this chapter is to describe transformational leadership behaviors that cause associates to accept responsibility for continually improving processes within the organization.

We do not presume that we can identify all of the leadership behaviors that contribute towards leadership effectiveness. However, we will identify those behaviors that we found to be effective when we spent three years in Florida's Department of Labor and Employment Security implementing an empowerment system. These behaviors were developed by continually monitoring the affects of specific leadership behaviors, and by surveying associates who were not at all timid about criticizing the behavior of leaders. We were fortunate in that we had over 7,000 associates and six divisions to observe and survey.

Without question, the number one criticism of leaders by associates was their behavior. We found that many government administrators either strongly resisted empowerment systems and/or did not know how to behave when lower-level members of the organization were empowered to improve the system. In this chapter, we will compare and contrast the behavior of effective transformational leaders and traditional administrators who cling to the belief that they do the thinking, and employees "do what they are told to do."

POWER AND ORGANIZATIONAL BEHAVIOR

Administrators in government bureaucracies often hold steadfast to traditional leadership beliefs, since they work in a system where authority is substituted for power. By holding a certain position in the organization, the administrator is vested with the authority to exercise power over subordinates. The position itself is sufficient to command subordinates and control their behavior. In such systems, personal characteristics of the leader are practically irrelevant. The position often has more credibility than the person holding it. Subordinates in bureaucracies learn to tolerate administrators in certain positions no matter what characteristics they may exhibit.

Two sources of power dominate government bureaucracies: position power and political power. If an administrator is fortunate to hold both position power and political power, subordinates, peers, and even superiors are of the opinion that the administrator is invulnerable no matter what leadership characteristics, skills, or behavior he or she exhibits. Practically anyone who has had any experience in working with government can identify incompetent administrators who have occupied the same position for years.

Power in government is primarily position power and has a strong influence on behavior. Subordinates grant authority to the position the administrator occupies and allow themselves to be controlled by rules and inept decisions. Because government employees tend to have a need for security and stability, they "fall in line," and although they may continually complain, they "go along to get along." Furthermore, government workers have had a history of routinely "kissing up" to political appointees who occupy very high positions in government. We have long admired the "staying power" of government administrators who, at a minimum of every four years, have to go through the ritual of impressing a new political appointee in order to maintain their positions. To offset position power, government workers not in key leadership jobs are somewhat protected by career service rules and regulations. This gives them some protection against administrators who abuse their position.

When position power is coupled with explicit bureaucratic goals, rules, and procedures, there is very little room for flexibility in the organization. It is easy to regulate the place of its members. Proponents of maintaining government organizations as they are would first grant to the leader the power needed "to lead." Second, they would advocate that the role of the leader is "to maintain the status quo" through the use of top-down management, rules, policies, and procedures to control behavior of workers.

If, indeed, all that is needed is position power coupled with rules, policies, and procedures, why bother with any management training? There would be no reason to develop the skills or characteristics of effective leaders. They would merely control the behavior of their subordinates by rules, policies, and procedures. With this power, they instinctively know the best thing to do and have the power to get it done, so why develop leadership skills?

Although we recognize the positive contribution of government organizations, we believe that government can significantly increase efficiency and effectiveness by developing systems that empower the work force and meet its needs. A cynic may argue that the government bureaucracy meets the needs of its administrators and workers through a paycheck and security, but not the needs of the customers it is supposed to serve. This may be a valid observation in the traditional bureaucracies. However, in a quality-driven agency that is concerned with customer satisfaction, and which has empowered associates to constantly improve processes, this is not true. Although people have a need for a paycheck and job security, their individual needs for achievement, growth, and self-worth are vitally important to them. An empowering agency meets all needs and rewards creativity, energy, motivation, and excellence.

EMPOWERMENT AND ORGANIZATIONAL BEHAVIOR

Bureaucratic systems that substitute authority for power discourage, or even prevent, the workforce from unleashing human potential. In fact, they often prevent natural, instinctive drives to improve the organization within an individual from occurring. Position power leaders frequently fail to maximize the potential of their followers because they fail to provide organizational leadership that motivates an individual to use brain power for the purpose of improving organization processes. Motivation is the inner drive that energizes and directs human behavior.

Motives for behavior stem primarily from two sources: internal (within the individual) and external (events in the environment). Position power leaders rely on external motivators to control their subordinates. They may make it clear that they can "write up" poor performers, add more work to their assignment, and withhold or grant pay raises. They enjoy preying on employees who are insecure or who suffer from a poor self-image. These leaders often assume that, left on their own, employees would be unable to perform effectively.

Individual behavior in organizations results from primary motives, i.e., motives that you are born with such as physiological and safety needs, and secondary motives, i.e., need for power, influence, achievement, money, rewards, status, etc. Understanding individual motives for a specific behavior is extremely difficult and complex. Sometimes, even the individual cannot identify what motivated a specific action.

Rather than dwelling on personal motives, organizations should pay little attention to analyzing individual motives and direct their energy towards understanding and developing systems that cause desirable behavior in the workplace. Organizational leaders who want to maximize the human potential of their workforce must be willing to share power and control in the work environment. They assume that associates are committed to their work when they are involved, and that they are capable of exercising self-direction and are eager to accept responsibility. They believe that they are capable of exhibiting creativity and ingenuity provided they are given the opportunity.

We have had the opportunity of testing these assumptions in government organizations and have found them to hold true. We never attempted to identify specific motives as to why any one individual elected to accept additional work and responsibilities when they were empowered to improve a process. All we know that as members of process improvement teams, they were willing and extremely capable of improving processes that had for years yielded poor, but acceptable, results.

We found that empowered associates are far more capable of improving organization performance than government administrators. In a later chapter, we will discuss some of the problems that will challenge leaders in implementing empowerment systems, since the journey is not an easy one and is "loaded with land mines." In this chapter, our focus is on associate behavior and leadership behavior.

Transformational leaders create an empowerment environment where information and power is shared, and where behavior is recognized, reinforced, and rewarded for the use of skills and abilities to improve the organization.

PERCEPTION AND BEHAVIOR

There are numerous articles describing how leaders should behave in organizations. These articles generally describe leadership behavior as "being all things to all people." They suggest, for example, that leaders are kind, loving, patient, never jealous, never boastful, never rude, never angry, and forgiving.

Although these behaviors sound good, they are inaccurate and unrealistic. Transformational leaders, for example, are sometimes patient, but occasionally grow tired of waiting for people in processes to change. Sometimes leaders even appear to be rude, raise their voices in anger, break the "golden rule," and appear to treat people worse than they would their enemies. Remember that if you are going to accept the responsibility of leadership, the perception of the behavior *is* the behavior to the person observing you. What a leader might believe is an act of kindness, another person might perceive as condescending. Helping people to lead themselves is not an easy task. In fact, it is often less work, and certainly less risky, to ignore them. One of the authors vividly remembers trying to help a team improve their processes and while doing so, engaged in an argument with one of its members. He had a great deal of respect for the team and particularly the team member with whom he was arguing. Even though he knew that other team members would take issue about the time and place of the argument, he continued on. Following the meeting, there was gossip throughout the halls on how he "had blasted" one of the team members. Some team members were even worried that the person with whom he was arguing, who was not afraid to speak his mind, would lose his job. The author knew exactly what he was doing. He wanted to assist the team in getting on track and show other team members that it was entirely acceptable to "take on the boss." By the next team meeting, the author had settled his differences with the member who spoke out, and the team began making progress. The problem was, however, that everyone on the team now enjoyed their new found freedom of arguing with a top administrator.

Obviously, conflicts should be avoided when possible, and effective leaders can often find alternative behaviors. However, transformational leaders are going to ruffle some feathers and sometimes be perceived as not being a "quality" person. To empower another person, however, means being authentic and honest, behavior which frequently arouses resistance and suspicion. This can cause attacks, not only from the person you are trying to help, but also from the individual's peers and friends. Therefore, the best judge of whether the leader is doing the right thing rests within that leader. If truly interested in empowering others, leaders will be far more interested in outcomes than they will be with initial perceptions.

When leaders put processes and people first, they sometimes suffer the consequences of being perceived inaccurately and may be the victims of harsh criticism. Many administrators are often far more concerned about themselves than they are others. Therefore, they are unwilling to take risks that may "shake" their perfect image. It is a lot less risky to stay in one's office and control subordinates than it is to work closely with them. However, transformational leaders are willing to take the risks since they find it extremely rewarding to help people lead themselves. If leaders are truly genuine in empowering others, they know that in the end they will be perceived accurately.

LEADING OTHERS TO LEAD THEMSELVES

On occasion, administrators in government complain about the quality of people who work for them. It is not uncommon to listen to two administrators argue over who has the worst workers. They wish for a change in the career service rules, so they could rid themselves of the poor workers. The reality is that if the people were as bad as described, administrators could dismiss them by documenting bad performance. Most administrators refuse to do the work required and are satisfied with maintaining the status quo even though they know that their work force is inefficient and ineffective. They also have a personal reason. Often, they are also members of the same career service system, and if cases for terminating people on poor performance were justified, they might also be caught in the same trap.

Administrators who are marking time in their jobs and are willing to maintain the status quo are soon discovered. All one needs to do is suggest a few ways they could help their poorly performing staff change. New ideas, i.e., improving their processes by treating their subordinates differently, are often met with resistance. It is interesting that so many government administrators blame their subordinates for being "unwilling to change," and then when asked to change their leadership approach, they respond with identical resistance.

If government is going to become efficient and effective, leaders are going to have to make dramatic changes in the way they lead. We believe that just as American industry eventually learned, the answer to efficiency and effectiveness in government resides in the work force. Government today is fortunate in that there are many leaders who recognize that we can have a quality government if we change our leadership approach. They recognize that organization success emulates from the bottom of the organization, but also recognize that there will be little change in government unless leaders at the top understand that their role is to lead others to lead themselves.

Transformational leadership starts with leaders who must be willing to change. They must think of their associates as able and capable people who can be trusted. Empowering leaders must be willing to grant them the authority and responsibility to initiate changes that improve government organizations. When this concept was first suggested to a number of administrators in Florida's Department of Labor and Employment Security, an immediate response was that if their subordinates "learned to manage themselves," there would be no need for administrators.

We had to agree with them if they continued to perceive of themselves as administrators. However, if administrators were to change their perspective and accept the role of being transformational leaders, they would find a big demand for their services. There is always plenty of work for transformational leaders, since they are continually working to improve people and processes. There is always a need in any organization for leaders who possess empowerment characteristics and skills and have the ability to develop the skills and abilities of others. If government changes the way it manages, however, there will be very little need for traditional administrators.

Transformational leaders recognize people for what they can do, not what they cannot do. They are willing to make a personal commitment to developing others and improving processes. They understand that their personal behavior is the key to empowering others. They are willing to embrace and adopt the following be-haviors:

1. Leading "by example."

Government administrators have been able to survive to a nice retirement, even though their philosophy might have been, "do as I say, not as I do." Transformational leaders cannot afford that luxury. In fact, one of the drawbacks to transformational leader-ship may be that the desired behaviors must be modeled con-stantly . Leaders cannot expect others to focus on customers when they focus only on themselves. They cannot expect others to col-lect, analyze, and use data for decision making if they ignore data. They cannot expect others to work in teams and not be on a team themselves. Leaders cannot expect others to flowchart and man-age processes if leaders continue to manage functions. Leaders must take the position that associates "do as you do."

"Walking the talk" is a requirement of transformational lead-ership. It doesn't mean that everyone in the organization will perceive you as "walking the talk," since people's perceptions differ significantly. In the long run, however, the vast majority of people, especially those with whom you work, will know that you are sincere in your efforts to empower them. They will observe you as you help them to meet or exceed customer expectations, as you help them analyze and collect data, as you help them make continual improvements in your process, etc. They know that you respect the organization values, since you try to model them daily.

Transformational leaders are hard workers. They are proactive and out front. They are the first to get to work in the morning and are genuinely excited about continually improving the organiza-tion. There is always ample work to be done. In fact, it seems as though there are not enough hours in the day to review data, work with teams, and recognize their accomplishments.

Transformational leaders see problems as opportunities for improvement. They are in constant dialogue with the people they want to empower. They increase their own self-image by improving the self-image of others. To be effective in helping others to lead themselves requires role modeling the desired behaviors.

2. Developing people.

Granting authority and responsibilities to associates to improve processes without developing their skills, will frequently yield poor results. There are two distinct developmental approaches a leader can take in developing associates. One approach is to teach them all of the skills that they will need prior to implementing process improvement. Another approach is called "just-in-time," where the leader empowers a process improvement team, and then teaches team members the knowledge and skills required for process improvement while they are actually working to improve their processes. We have tried both approaches and found each has certain advantages.

By teaching associates the knowledge and skills they need prior to implementing teams, you get them prepared for what they are about to do. A disadvantage to this approach is that associates fail to comprehend much of what is taught, since they are unable to apply it to a real situation. When you teach associates knowledge and skills prior to implementation, you may have to retrain them again. On the other hand, "just in time" training deals with real problems and opportunities. It seems to be more effective.

Whatever approach a leader takes, there will be confusion. It is not easy to ask people who have been "doing what they have been told to do" to think about their work in a significantly different way. When you first begin to empower associates, you have to be willing to endure criticism and have a high tolerance for uncertainty.

Transformational leaders view each associate as a valuable resource and therefore, are willing to expend significant effort in helping them learn to manage themselves and their processes. Each person and each team is a project in itself. That is why we believe that every transformational leader must be an effective teacher. Leaders have to develop their associates in all of the skills that were usually reserved for management. This requires considerable work.

Leaders have to show associates how to gather data regarding customers, suppliers, and their processes. They have to be shown how to flowchart their processes, how to use data in making decisions, how to work effectively in teams, and even how to make effective presentations.

Frequently administrators believe that they can delegate training and development to their human resources staff. Although human resources can be extremely helpful to a transformational leader, transformational leaders accept the responsibility for the development of their people. Many human resources trainers are more concerned about the evaluations they receive when conducting seminars than they are about outcomes. They know that if they want to receive high evaluations, particularly from managers, they need to let the people being trained monopolize the seminar. Many government administrators like to go to seminars where they can voice their philosophy, rather than learn a new philosophy. Quality indicators for a training program should focus more on outcomes, instead of simple evaluations indicating whether a person enjoyed being at the seminar. It is far more important that trainees leave the seminar understanding and adopting the concepts taught.

Transformational leaders understand that human resources can make a significant contribution in their empowerment efforts, but also accept the responsibility for the training of their associates by regularly participating as instructors. In this manner, they help assure outcomes.

3. Initiating structure.

Administrators have long recognized the importance of establishing structure in directing subordinates. Structure defines the role of the administrator and the roles of subordinates in attaining goals. The role of the administrator is to establish deadlines, make assignments, and maintain standards of performance. The role of subordinates is to follow procedures and to see that their work meets the standards. Structure is an important leadership dimension, and transformational leaders understand that without structure, processes can go awry. One important difference between traditional administration and transformational leadership is that transformational leaders ensure structure by enabling workers closest to the work to structure their work activities. This does not mean that transformational leaders do not have a high concern for structure. On the contrary, they have a high need for the process to be performed; however, they empower their work force to structure how work should be done. Transformational leaders allow work teams to coordinate activities instead of planning and scheduling the work themselves.

Transformational leaders initiate structure by working with teams to establish quality goals, quality indicators, and work activities. Planning, coordinating, and organizing operations are shared responsibilities. Although empowered teams accept the primary responsibility for initiating structure, transformational leaders empower and train teams to structure their work effectively.

4. Providing consideration and support.

Very few people enjoy working for a leader who doesn't show support and consideration. Associates appreciate a leader who looks out for their welfare. Government administrators have understood the importance of this dimension and frequently assure subordinates that they are looking out for their "best interest." To prove themselves in this dimension, administrators communicate to subordinates how they protect them from attacks by upper management. In fact, government administrators are extremely effective in convincing subordinates that they have their best interest at heart. When administrators successfully convince them of this protection and support, the administrator expects loyalty in return from subordinates.

It is amazing how many subordinates become "trapped" by government administrators in this game. Administrators withhold information from subordinates, and only tell them stories about how they "protected" them during meetings. It is not uncommon for administrators to return from a meeting with upper management to say very little about what occurred. They select the right information to pass on, proving support and demonstrating they were sensitive to, and considerate of, the subordinate's welfare.

Transformational leaders take a different approach. They show support and consideration by sharing all vital information with subordinates. They believe in their subordinates and trust their performance. They realize that the best protection is doing effective work. Furthermore, they believe that support and consideration are best achieved by helping subordinates develop themselves and their team. One of the most effective methods for developing consideration and support is to take a genuine interest in the development of people and to behave, when appropriate, in a friendly, positive and appreciative manner.

5. Making decisions.

Many administrators in government claim that their job is hard because they are constantly saddled with tough decisions. We have observed a number of administrators complain that they are "stressed out" because they are overwhelmed by the amount of work they have to do and the difficult decisions they have to make daily. Although we believe that transformational leaders need to be tough, i.e., to endure the "onslaught of hits" by associates who resist empowerment systems, decision making does not require a transformational leader to be tough-minded.

In fact, when empowerment systems function effectively, decision making is a very enjoyable task. From time to time, a transformational leader may have to deal with associate behavior that is interfering with the achievement of team and organizational goals. However, most of the time transformational leaders are allowing project and process improvement teams to make decisions. Furthermore, decision making is a relatively easy process when quality data drives the decision. When scientific methods are employed by teams, decision making is not difficult. Since transformational leaders are members of both project and process improvement teams, they will experience the enjoyment of making decisions that will be tested to see if they are correct.

It is important to remember that process improvement decisions are always productive, even when they do not work. Transformational leaders adopt the philosophy of Thomas Edison, the great inventor, who told a visitor to his laboratory that he had to find ten thousand ways the light bulb would not work before he finally found the right way. Each "failure" was a step in the direction of a successful outcome.

6. Planing strategically.

Government administrators fully understand that one of their functions is to develop the annual plan that drives human behavior. Once the plan is in place, it is the administrator's job to see that it is carefully followed. There is a presumed direct correlation between "the plan" and performance. The failure of this management practice became blatantly clear to one of the authors who had the opportunity to visit the Soviet Union prior to the demise of the Berlin wall. Each year, Kremlin party leaders came together to develop plans for the following year and to develop five-year plans. They would determine what was needed, set objectives and quotas, and then outline what steps would be taken to complete the plan. Their assumption was that if everyone followed the plan, the country would be successful. Once the plan was put into effect, no one was allowed to change it or improve it. The results of such a management system was, of course, disastrous. Millions of people suffered because the Kremlin leaders never understood the concept of empowerment.

Transformational leaders understand that strategic plans provide direction. They set the course of action, but empower associates to make changes and improvements that help the organization go in the direction it desires. Transformational leaders accept strategic planning as their responsibility and are willing to meet regularly with their strategic planning team to review and improve their plan.

7. Emphasizing processes.

Government administrators emphasize the function of control. The problem with most administrators, however, is that they believe that it is their job to control people. Transformational leaders, on the other hand, are far more interested in how their process functions, as opposed to how people function. Transformational leaders leave the selection of a specific behavior to their associates, while administrators are often bent on controlling associate behavior. Since transformational leaders attend to the process, they frequently challenge the process by asking questions. They ask challenging and difficult questions regarding the processes they lead, and take genuine interest in data that emerges from process measurement. They are competent in using continual improvement tools and work closely with process improvement teams in using these tools to make improvements. At times when teams get bogged down, transformational leaders exercise their facilitation skills, since they understand how work flows within the process and have a good grasp of quality indicator data. They can become very effective in assisting their associates to improve and control their processes.

8. Empowering teams.

Government administrators rely heavily on their position and self-proclaimed knowledge to improve productivity. They believe it is their job to know what needs to be done. It's been said that some administrators plead with team members not to report exciting process improvement changes, for fear that upper management may question why the administrator did not think of the ideas first.

Transformational leaders take the opposite point of view. They are excited when their team generates an idea that improves a process. Transformational leaders empower their associates by granting them the authority and responsibility for continual improvement. One of the most effective approaches to empower associates is to form teams that are assigned to a specific process. The teams are then asked to meet for one hour each week to review their processes. Each team is responsible for establishing their mission and values, flowcharting and measuring their process, and making continual improvements. (For a complete description of how to empower teams, see *Teams in Government* [1996], by Jerry W. Koehler and Joseph M. Pankowski, published by St. Lucie Press, Delray Beach, FL).

9. Recognizing and rewarding associates.

Government administrators understand the importance of recognition and rewards. Most, however, complain about the lack of recognition given by upper management to them and to their subordinates. Furthermore, they often tell you that they could personally improve their performance and the performance of their subordinates if government merely increased salaries. Rarely do you attend a meeting of government leaders and front-line associates without hearing about how poorly everyone is paid. Transformational leaders may share the same feelings about pay; however, this does not prevent them from effective leadership. They understand the attitudes of their associates and realize that they must increase their efforts to recognize and reward associates. It requires them to attend to reward and recognition behavior daily. They visit teams, make short presentations of appreciation, give certificates and plaques and generate thoughtful remarks about associates and the quality of their work. In Florida's Department of Labor and Employment Security, we developed criteria for both leadership and team awards. We encouraged associates to strive for these awards, and found it very exciting to hear team presentations and to listen to associates nominate their associates for leadership awards. We found it interesting that even though administrators complained about recognition and rewards, many refused to encourage their teams to apply for recognition. On the other hand, transformational leaders took great pride in listening to their empowered teams make a presentation. Below is the criteria we used for the team award and the leadership award.

Criteria for Team Awards

Impact of change

Describe the actual impact of the change. How are customers better served as a result of this change? Examples might include improved productivity (i.e., shorter waiting lines for our customers), lower costs, happier customers, better quality jobs for our customers (both external and internal), increased status of our programs in the community, "thank you" letters from our customers, etc. Provide actual data, including charts whenever feasible.

Process supports mission, goals, and values

Describe how the change supports the goal, mission, and values of the department. The improved process should relate directly to one of these with a description that clearly demonstrates this connection. For example, one component of the department's mission is to help return to work those individuals who have experienced injuries while working and almost any improvement in the workers' compensation program could be attributed to this part of the mission.

Team participation

Describe how team members were selected and how roles and responsibilities of each member were decided. Did the team clearly understand its purpose and was it empowered to create change? Provide evidence. How was consensus reached on assignments of work to be done? Provide evidence of cohesiveness, trust, open communication, mutual support, and empowerment.

Customer feedback

Describe how the team determined who was its customers and what were their needs? Were customer surveys well designed so that customers had little difficulty expressing their concerns? Include a brief description of methods and measurement scales used, including frequency of customer contact.

Ongoing improvements (future plans)

Describe how the team may continue to address future improvements in the process. No process is static, and improvements are always possible. For example, a future improvement may be in a sub-component of the previous process identified. Once the suggested improvement is implemented, the team may find additional refinements or changes in policy that will improve the process even more. These future plans should be presented.

Identified/documented process

Describe how the team defined the problem and identified the process to study. How was the process charted and studied? Did team members complete a flowchart working together and was there agreement by all? Include a copy of the process flowchart and any other documentation tools used.

Quality data

Describe how and why data was selected and collected. Include discussion of any special collection efforts related to customer satisfaction (i.e., mail surveys, telephone calls, visits to individual customers, focus groups, complaint letters, etc.). Also include any reports or special studies (government, etc.) that were used by the team. Was any of the data used developed within the department or was any purchased outside? Were team members assigned responsibility for collecting any data? How were samples selected? How did the team try to ensure that the data was reliable?

Use of quality tools

Describe how the team used the quality improvement tools (flowcharts, cause and effect diagrams, histograms, Pareto charts, scatterplots, run charts, control charts, etc.). How did the team decide which tools were most appropriate? Attach copies of graphs and charts used by the team.

Linked process to other processes

Describe how the team justified how the improved process is linked to other processes that will be impacted by the improvements made. For example, an improvement may be made in a process without direct impact on customer satisfaction, and yet through linkage, it may have a profound impact on another process that does. How does the improved process fit into the global picture (linked to other processes)?

Level of risk involved

Describe the level of risk assumed by the team in its study and improvement of the selected process. For example, a process improvement that identifies top management as a prime cause of a bottleneck in grant review may be perceived as more risky than identifying a problem in the mail room. Although this is not true in an organization committed to customer satisfaction, there is still the perception that suggestions involving executive problems are more risky. Another risky improvement may call for a personnel or legislative action that may not please everyone.

Leadership Criteria

Role Modeling of Values

Demonstrates the agreed-upon values of the organization in word and deed.

Process Management

Focuses on the way work gets done, on the organization of people, procedures, equipment, and puts energy into work activities for the purposes of process optimization. Identifies core processes, recruits teams, leads team analysis, flowcharts processes, detects and removes causes of variation, and measures the effects on customers.

Quality Tools and Data

Uses quality tools and data in managing the daily operation of his or her organization. Encourages and helps associates to receive training in quality tools and data, including serving as a training resource when necessary.

Linkages

Demonstrates knowledge of customers affected by his or her process. Understands and can explain the relationships between his or her process and other affected processes/customers.

Customer Focus

Consistently aims his or her work at meeting or exceeding customer expectations. Recognizes both external customers (those who use and benefit from services offered), and internal customers (those fellow associates whose work depends on the work that precedes them). Continually solicits feedback from customers through conversation, observation, and surveys/questionnaires.

Empowerment

Involves others by sharing information and power. Advocates and participates in team-driven policy determination, whereby front-line associates who directly serve customers are entrusted to drive policy for their processes based on the data they have collected and analyzed. Actively works to reduce internal and external barriers that hinder performance. Encourages associates' creativity.

Recognition

Provides encouragement and support for associates' participation in continual quality improvements by communicating their efforts and successes through verbal, written, and ceremonial expressions of praise.

Communication

Clearly and consistently communicates the quality message to associates and customers. Facilitates the gathering and sharing of information with the intent to improve customer service. Solicits information from customers and associates about his or her processes and any improvements that can be made.

Training

Demonstrates knowledge of TQM concepts, attends TQM training, facilitates TQM training availability to associates, encourages/supports their participation, and enhances others' understanding of TQM concepts through daily interactions.

Risk Taking

Accepts the risk of disapproval and the other negative consequences that may result from the active pursuit of continual process improvement.

Each criterion has a maximum potential score of 10. A "perfect score" is 100 points. A leadership nominee must receive at least 80 points, based on the average for all Quality Council members' scores, to qualify for a leadership award.

10. Assesses performance.

Evaluating the performance of subordinates is an annual event for government administrators. Many administrators use the annual performance review as their primary means to control subordinates. They establish criteria and annually evaluate subordinates against this criteria. Since the performance and the performance review is often considered a control mechanism, position power administrators realize that it can be a powerful weapon in their arsenal. Some cannot wait for the annual performance review to "get" subordinates who don't follow their directions precisely.

For transformational leaders, the annual performance review is just another job requirement. It is not used as a significant control mechanism, but rather it is perceived as an opportunity to help associates to personally improve their performance. In fact, it can be a very positive and rewarding experience for both the leader and the associate. From time to time, transformational leaders will find an associate who is working against process improvement and will be judged to be of little value to the organization. In this case, transformational leaders are not afraid to honesty communicate to the subordinate that their performance is not acceptable.

In most cases, the annual performance review will be extremely positive since transformational leaders do not wait until the annual performance review to work with associates to improve their performance. The transformational leader goes directly to subordinates and works with them when performance is not meeting or exceeding expectations. Usually the leader is successful.

We have observed organizations that adopt the policy where administrators were told that they had to follow a prescribed rule in evaluating their subordinates. For example, one organization only allowed administrators to evaluate one-third of their subordinates as exceeding expectations. Transformational leaders realize this is ridiculous. An effective transformational leader should have everyone in the unit exceeding expectations. Effective leadership causes exceptional performance, and therefore, it is acceptable for a transformational leader to positively manage the performance of all associates by giving them the excellent ratings they have earned.

SUMMARY

The behavior of a transformational leader is the key variable to improving government organization. It requires a person with empowerment characteristics and skills who is motivated and dedicated to continual improvement. It requires a person who is not afraid to be out front, to be proactive, to be involved, and to be highly visible. It requires a leader who leads by example, develops people, initiates structure, provides consideration and support, makes decisions, plans strategically, emphasizes processes, empowers teams, recognizes and rewards associates, and assesses performance.

Furthermore, transformational leaders are willing to "walk the talk" and get into the trenches working side by side with their associates to improve organizational performance. The behavior of transformational leaders makes a significant difference in the organization.

CHAPTER 7

TRANSFORMATIONAL LEADERSHIP: SUBSTITUTES

When we were trying to implement transformational leadership in the Department of Labor and Employment Security in Florida, we experienced monumental barriers created by administrators who were instrumental in presenting obstacles that nullified the effects of our leadership. These particular barriers, which limited the position power of a leader, were what Kerr and Jermier[1] refer to as "neutralizers." For example, when we asked administrators to empower teams to improve processes, we met resistance from administrators who were quick to point out that rules, regulations, and policy prevented the use of teams. Thus, they were able to neutralize our leadership.

In addition, we found that neutralizers also served as a substitute for effective management by administrators. In other words, the same rules, regulations, and policies that administrators were using to neutralize our attempts to make changes were also substitutes for administrative leadership. Administrators were unable to effectively lead since they were neutralized by rules, regulations, and policy. It was disheartening to discover that government administrators seemed to relish the fact that the same rules, regulations, and policies that prevented them from being effective leaders could also be used to prevent empowering systems. We have long been aware of the neutralizing influence of employee organizations, such as a strong labor union, which neutralizes the position power of leaders by taking away their power to reward and punish employees.

Government leaders have long complained that career service rules and regulations prevented them from doing the job that was required. Most administrators complained that the rules and policies are so inflexible that they prevent them from influencing subordinates. For example, financial rewards are often automatic and an employee will receive a specified percentage increase whether they are competently or incompetently performing their job.

We were prepared for this neutralizing affect; however, we were not prepared for administrators to use the neutralizing power of these same rules to prevent empowering front-line employees. It wasn't that front-line associates were as much opposed to empowerment systems as their administrators. In fact, most of the resistance to implementing empowerment systems emerged from administrators from the top of their divisions where we were attempting to implement empowerment systems. It was only after we spent countless hours of training top administrators on how to empower associates that we realized that they were going to be successful in neutralizing our attempts to influence them. Therefore, we needed to find another way to influence organization members to change. In other words, we had to find leader substitutes.

In a business organization that is financially in trouble, our strategy would be to replace managers with leaders who embraced transformational leadership. However, in government it would take forever to replace administrators since they would be able to use rules, regulations, and policies to neutralize our attempts to replace them. Therefore, we had to find substitutes, not actual replacements, for leaders who were constraining our efforts.

In our attempt to find these substitutes, we were able to begin to understand their importance for leadership in government organizations, even when transformational leaders embrace empowerment systems. We found that there are many factors positively influencing the behavior of associates that a transformational leader can rely on. In other words, transformational leaders do not need to invent new behaviors to empower others, but rather identify factors that strongly influence behavior which make leader endorsement and support unnecessary.

Traditional leadership approaches take the position that the leader is the primary supplier of influence. Transformational leadership, on the other hand, argues that behavior influence can be caused by many factors. In other words, the primary supplier to cause specific associate behavior does not have to be the leader. Transformational leaders use substitutes to influence the attitudes and behaviors of associates. It is the responsibility of transformational leaders to find substitutes for their leadership and implement them in the system.

It is important to understand that we are not suggesting there are substitutes for leadership, but rather that there are substitutes that make leadership behavior unnecessary. Leadership in the workplace is always a vital factor since there is always a need for leadership influence. However, specific leadership behaviors may not be required if substitutes are active in the workplace. In other words, government leaders continually influence the attitudes and behaviors of associates; however, they use specific factors found in empowerment systems to substitute for leadership behavior that normally would be required.

For example, a leader may strongly influence the design of a specific job. However, if the leader selects an individual for the job who knows more about the job requirements that anyone else, including the leader, then the leader can let the individual determine the best way to do the job. This gives the leader the freedom to attend to other leadership priorities, since an extremely qualified person has been found for the job and thus in effect, a leader "substitute" has been found.

We strongly believe that transformational leaders should constantly be searching for leader substitutes, especially in government where their attempts to influence followers are easily neutralized. Not only do effective substitutes reduce the need for government administrators, but they strongly influence the behavior of associates. They assist the leader in implementing empowerment systems and facilitate the delegation of authority. For example, when we were implementing Total Quality Management in the Department of Labor and Employment Security in Florida, we used leader substitutes to influence associates who were unfortunate enough to have administrators who strongly resisted TQM.

In our attempts to "submarine" resisting administrators by finding and implementing substitutes, we discovered leader substitutes to be essential in empowering systems. Although we focused on leader substitutes for a negative reason, we found that leader substitutes are natural and effective in empowerment systems. Leadership substitutes are extremely beneficial, even when administrators do not resist change. They often eliminate the necessity for many leader behaviors, since they provide direction and motivation for associates without a direct cause and effect relationship between leader behavior and follower response. In essence, they make a leader unnecessary in many situations.

Government bureaucracies with their explicit goals, rules, and procedures inherently provide leadership substitutes. The problem, however, is that these substitutes are antithetical to transformational leadership and empowerment systems. Rather than encouraging creativity and teamwork, they stifle them. Furthermore, they fail to tap the brain power of organizational members. Our search for leadership substitutes that are effective in empowerment systems led us to identify the following leadership substitutes.

1. Organization-wide compensation and recognition program.

When administrators resisted taking the lead in implementing Total Quality Management in Florida's Department of Labor and Employment Security, we instituted a program that proved to be extremely effective as a leadership substitute. We offered a bonus of as much as $1,000 for each team member who participated on a process improvement team, and who was willing to present their results to the Department's Quality Council. Compensation was a powerful substitution for leadership. When compensation was removed the following year, the number of teams appearing before the Quality Council was dramatically reduced.

To appear before the Quality Council, each team had to be nominated by their division. Therefore, before any team had appeared before the department's Quality Council, they had already been reviewed by their division and had acquired the division's sponsorship.

The Quality Council developed the criteria for team awards (identified in Chapter 6). We followed a similar process in how we set values. We first identified the criteria and then members of the Council volunteered to write a description of the criteria. We believe that each Quality Council should develop its own criteria. It helps the Council to better understand TQM and to have a thorough understanding of the criteria.

2. Cohesive process improvement teams.

One of our beliefs is that associates closest to the work being done are in the best position to improve it. Therefore, we empowered front-line work teams to improve their processes. For example, after we merged unemployment and job services within Florida's Department of Labor and Employment Security, we empowered front-line teams to improve the process. Many administrators strongly resented these teams. They predicted failure and chaos. Since we believed that cohesive work teams would provide a substitute for leadership, we asked these administrators to give as much support as they could or, at a minimum, not to interfere with the teams.

Our assumption proved to be correct. Cohesive work teams did not require the assistance of a leader. This is not to say or suggest that one can just remove an administrator and turn the work over to subordinates. We did find that in some cases where teams were unable to perform as a cohesive unit, something short of chaos occurred. However, when teams cohesively focused on the customers of their process, used data to make their decisions and were empowered to change the process, it made administrators unnecessary.

3. Process improvement guides.

Teams often experience significant difficulty in getting started and keeping their momentum. Significant obstacles occur that require more than just a facilitator, e.g., an individual who works with top management and process improvement teams. These individuals are effective leadership substitutes and can be designated as process improvement guides (PIGs). They are given the responsibility to help team members in the group process by (1) observing and evaluating how the team is functioning, (2) providing training in team dynamics and the teachings of the quality improvement "gurus" as needed, (3) helping select appropriate "tools" for teams to use, and (4) helping the teams prepare presentations for the Quality Council. The concept of the process improvement guide was a highly successful one and proved to be an effective leadership substitute.

4. Professional workforce.

An effective leadership substitute is a well-trained and mature workforce. In traditional organizations, once a person has performed a task for a considerable time, leadership is often unnecessary. In empowerment organizations, job tasks are not always simple and repetitive. In fact, it is everyone's responsibility to participate in teams for the purpose of improving processes.

Consequently, every person in an empowerment system must be well trained in numerous skills. In a sense, everyone is a professional. In Florida's Department of Labor and Employment Security, we referred to them as quality professionals. They were trained in how to analyze customer needs and expectations, how to use quality tools, how to participate in teams effectively, and how to manage their processes. Front-liners were considered professionals. Professionals are associates who understand how to set goals, how to plan for improvement, how to organize their work, how to control their processes, how to make decisions, how to participate in meetings, how to analyze data, how to chart data, how to make effective presentations, how to flowchart processes, how to resolve conflicts in teams, etc. The more professional the workforce, the less leadership behavior is required.

5. Mission identification, understanding, and acceptance.

It has been very popular recently for organizations to establish mission statements and to publicize them in numerous ways. The problem is, however, that most mission statements remain just words. Thus associates fail to understand and attach meaning to the mission. We found that once understood, believed, and accepted by associates, a mission statement becomes a powerful substitute for leadership.

For example, although our mission in the Department of Labor and Employment Security was to "return people to work," we found a number of our divisions who thought their mission was only to provide "benefits" to their customers. When we tried to persuade associates to adopt the mission, we met resistance. They were so ingrained with their specific job tasks that it was difficult to convince them that it wasn't their job to provide benefits, but to help their customers return to work.

If an associate did not identify, understand, and accept the mission of our department as their own, they required substantial leadership. A leader would have to work with these associates every day to change their mind set. However, when the mission was accepted by associates, they were able to direct their own behavior. Too often organizations overlook the impact of a mission statement and treat it more as an ornament than as a leadership substitute. Establishing the mission and, more important, ingraining the mission in the minds of the workforce is extremely important.

6. Instilling values.

Along with mission statements, it is common to find published values in organizations. Values are important since they guide the behavior of organization members. The problem with most value statements is just that, they remain "a statement." Very few administrators embrace them. Many administrators believe that they can ignore them and continue to use their position power to control subordinates.

Most administrators probably do not know why they resist organizational values, even though they find very little fault with them. They unconsciously reject organization-wide values as an important dimension within their organization because values often interfere with their ability to manipulate subordinate behavior. For example, if an organization has adopted "trust" or "open and honest communication" as a value, some administrators would find that practicing this value would detract from their power to manipulate subordinates. Another example could be "teamwork." Although some administrators claim to be team builders, they reject the notion that subordinates can be as resourceful or even more resourceful than an administrator.

If organization-wide values are instilled in all members, rules and regulations become less important. While rules and regulations frequently restrict behavior, values instill creativity, honesty, candor, respect, innovation, and openness. They provide direction to associates in selecting positive organization behavior and allow transformational leaders the freedom to use their creative and innovative skills.

7. Quality indicators.

When we would attend an organizational review conducted by legislators and legislative staff, we were frequently amazed by how little they understood our processes. This may have been due to the number of agencies they were reviewing, the frequent "turnover" in legislative positions, or even our own inability to communicate to them. Invariably, one or two legislators would inform us how "poorly" our agency treated one of their constituents. Furthermore, they would lecture us on how we should "do better" in the future if we were going to receive more funding.

After they embarrassed us with their questions, their stern looks, and a reminder that they were in power, they would show their ignorance by focusing on goals and quotas. Little did they know that they were falling right into our trap, since we were an extremely effective organization when the only measurements were goals and quotas. After all, we set the goals and quotas and since we were not stupid, we set goals and quotas that we could easily attain. And if for some reason we did not meet a specific goal, we were loaded with excuses, showing that it was not our fault.

What the legislators and their staff missed was that they were not able to determine whether or not we were a quality organization. Since they did not understand quality, they could and did annually fund programs that may not benefit their constituents. They had no idea how they could measure quality. They only measured output. At least some legislatures and their staffs are now beginning to focus on outcomes as opposed to just output. Outcomes may be a step in the right direction, but until legislatures and their staffs focus on quality indicators, they will not be able to effectively manage government.

Quality indicators are measures that best represent the factors that lead to improved customer, operational, and asset performance. These measures track service quality and show how the organization is achieving its mission. For example, quality measures in the Division of Unemployment Compensation had the following quality indicators:

- Customer Service Surveys

- Number of Claims Filed

- Initial Claims Quality

- Job Service Registration

- Timely Input of Initial Claims

- First Payment Time Lapse

- Voice Processing System

- Monetary Redeterminations

- Nonmonetary Quality

- Nonmonetary Timeliness

- Percent of Appeals Reversals

- Eligibility Reviews Performed

- Issues Detected for Eligibility Reviews

- Benefit Quality Control Error Rate

- Overpayment Determinations Issued

- Overpayment Dollars Determined

- Overpayment Dollars Recovered

- Overpayment Recovery Rate

- Fraud Investigation Timeliness

- B.P.C. Examiner vs. Automatic Determined Dollars

- Double By-Pass Adjudication Distribution

- Warrants Determined Undeliverable

- Average Weekly Duration of Claims

- Amount of Benefits Paid

- Total Number of Weeks of Benefits Paid

- New Hires

- RSVP Customers

Administrators are often reluctant to identify and measure quality indicators. They are afraid to expose their dirty laundry to legislators and newspapers. However, transformational leaders take the position that the only way the organization can improve is for everyone, primarily their organizational members, to understand the results of their quality initiative. Determining what actually is occurring in the organization is a vital step for continual improvement. Furthermore, when all of the members of an organization can identify how they are being measured, they are motivated to take steps that will improve results. They "buy into" doing their share to improve the organization. These indicators become very important to them, and they do not need position power administrators to control them. We were overwhelmed by the number of associates in Florida's Department of Labor and Employment Security who didn't even know the error rate in their office. However, when they found out that the error rate was an important indicator, most of the associates had the desire to drive down the error rate. Quality indicators are an effective leadership substitute.

8. 360-degree feedback systems.

Organizations have had to traditionally use the administrator-subordinate system to provide feedback to subordinates. The administrator observed the work and then provided positive reinforcement or constructive criticism to improve the performance of the subordinate. The problem with this system is that it only provides information from one source, and it often produces confrontations and grievances when the information is negative.

A far more effective method for helping organizations to improve is to design a system where not only the administrator, but peers and customers provide feedback to the associates. With this approach, associates understand that they do not just work for an administrator and that it is important to develop effective relationships with all the people with whom they interact. The "360-degree feedback system" is a valuable tool for transformational leaders. Rather than being the only source for evaluating the behavior of a subordinate, they rely on many other sources for assistance in developing and evaluating subordinates.

9. Process measurement, control and benchmarking.

Administrators spend much of their time trying to control the behavior of their subordinates and often expend considerable physical and intellectual energy anticipating their next move in this attempt. Transformational leaders, on the other hand, can logically assume that if the processes to which they are assigned are in control, they can spend less time worrying about the behavior of their subordinates. While traditional administrators assign tasks to subordinates, transformational leaders empower teams to improve processes. While traditional administrators try to assign blame for not meeting expectations, transformational leaders grant authority and responsibility to the team to meet or exceed customers' expectations in their assigned process.

Team members look to facts and data for direction. The data collected by the team reveals information that causes specific actions of team members. In other words, facts, data, and analysis direct the behavior of associates. Measurement and control of a process thus becomes a leadership substitute. An important part of measurement and control is to focus on improving measures that have a direct relationship to meeting or exceeding customer expectations. We believe the old saying, "what gets measured gets done!"

Benchmarking processes, i.e., comparing your processes to the "best practices," helps the team to determine the effectiveness of their process. Rather than an administrator trying to assess individual performance, the team assesses process performance by comparing their process to the best. Benchmarking is a way of comparing your processes to those of a recognized leader and of identifying gaps. If you know where you are in respect to those who compete with you, it may be possible to study your processes to see how they can be improved to exceed the competition.

A good example of benchmarking can be found in the Xerox experience. For years Xerox led the world in the manufacture of superb copiers. Yet, when competition heated up from copier manufacturers in Japan, it was evident that to stay competitive, Xerox had to intensify its efforts to be the best. They implemented benchmarking.

Benchmarking consists of a series of several steps. First, identify the subject and key characteristics of the benchmarking. For example, an agency interested in accurate eligibility decisions for disability insurance based upon criteria set by the federal government, might use an error rate supplied by the Social Security Administration. Then, identify who will be benchmarked—other agencies, companies, or organizations—and collect data. In our example above, we would likely select agencies in other states performing the same work. We would look for "the best" or those whose error rates are lower than ours. Analyze the reasons for the gap that exists between your program and the best. Examine your processes (using teams who do the work) to see where improvements can be made. Examine what the best does that makes it the best. Constantly improve and examine your processes.

10. Organization effectiveness criteria.

In 1994, we were looking for a way to honor and recognize the Division of Unemployment Compensation for the remarkable improvements made by their associates. We encouraged the Division to apply for the Sterling Award, which has criteria similar to the nationally recognized Baldridge Award. Although the Division qualified for a site visit (the first government entity in Florida to be chosen), the division did not win the award.

However, the effects of applying for the award were much stronger than we had imagined. The site visit was itself very rewarding, but more importantly, applying for the award and using the criteria to measure our organization's effectiveness were extremely beneficial.

The criteria for the award is based upon a set of quality excellence standards and addresses all key requirements to achieve quality focusing not only on results, but also on conditions and processes that lead to results. The criteria offers a framework that organizations can use to tailor their systems and processes toward continually improving quality performance. This is a leadership substitute, since it signals to the associate the criteria for organization effectiveness. It empowers associates since it clearly defines their roles and responsibilities. For example, the award criteria is based upon concepts which represent the underlying basis for integrating the overall customer and organization operational performance requirements.

The system for scoring organization effectiveness is based upon three evaluation dimensions: (1) approach, (2) deployment, and (3) results. The approach refers to how the organization addresses the methods they use, deployment refers to the extent to which the organization's approach is applied to all requirements, and results refer to outcomes in achieving the purpose.

For example, if an organization was to be judged on the effectiveness of strategic planning, examiners would evaluate this item relative to approach, deployment, and results. If the organization received the highest score for this item, their approach would have to meet the following criteria: "prevention and fact-based quality systems are fully responsive to all the purposes of strategic planning with continuous evaluation and improvement cycles and substantial refinements." Regarding the deployment, the criteria states, "approach is fully deployed to all units with no gaps in deployment" and "all work units are in the advanced stages of advancement." And finally, regarding results, the criteria calls for "excellent (world-class) results and strong, sustained trends in all areas important to strategic planning and key organization factors" and "strong evidence of benchmark leadership."

Organization criteria categories are as follows:

- Leadership

- Information and analysis

- Strategic planning

- Human resource excellence

- Process management

- Performance results

- Customer focus and satisfaction

Leadership drives the four system categories: process management, human resource excellence, strategic planning, and information analysis. These four systems along with leadership are aimed at meeting or exceeding customer expectations and performance results.

What makes effective organization criteria so powerful as a leadership substitute is that every process comes under scrutiny. Associates are required to assess their processes against organization criteria. It helps them to focus on what work is important and how workflow should be processed. It makes them examine key customer requirements, the role of the supplier, and the way they can participate in improving their organization.

Endnotes

1. S. Kerr and J.M. Jermier. "Substitutes for Leadership: Their Meaning and Measurement." *Organizational Behavior and Human Performance,* 22(1978): 375–403.

CHAPTER 8

TRANSFORMATIONAL LEADERSHIP: INSPIRING CHANGE

"There is nothing more difficult to take in hand, more perilous to conduct, or more uncertain in its success, than to take the lead in the introduction of a new order of things."

—Niccolo Machiavelli, *The Prince*

It is difficult to imagine a leader in today's government who is not advocating change. Many external environmental forces, such as economics, technology, and even governmental regulations are having a profound impact on government. Legislators, taxpayers, and government customers are crying for government to be more efficient and effective. Furthermore, business and industry have made dramatic changes in the way they manage their resources, and people are asking government to follow their example.

Internal forces within government are also having a profound affect. With fewer resources, government workers realize that they must do more with less. They understand that jobs need to be restructured and new management systems need to be developed. They also know that if an organization is going to be efficient and effective, the workforce must be deployed more effectively. They realize the impact of technology and understand that their role in the workplace is going to change significantly. They know the bureaucracy that was so carefully designed to isolate tasks and responsibilities has proven to be an antiquated system. They realize that change must occur.

NEED FOR A CHANGE

In 1990, we were asked to lead a major change initiative in Florida's Department of Labor and Employment Security. Our job was to implement Total Quality Management within the department. Like most government organizations, change was not uncommon. Associates in the department frequently complained they were asked to change every time they inherited a "new administration." For the most part, the associates in the department were not affected by changes of the new administration. They learned how to cope with change over the years, and in most cases continued to do business as usual, except to give the appearance that they were "going along" with new change initiatives. Although most change was "revolutionary" and required training and new skills, the alterations generally did not threaten the existing culture. The restructuring of the organization and the implementation of new policies were not dramatic and did little to upset the work force.

We wanted to accomplish, however, radical change. We advocated new beliefs, values, and management systems that caused associates to rethink how they would go about their daily business of doing things. We did not go so far as to request that associates reinvent government. However, we asked associates to adopt beliefs, values, and principles that led to incremental change. We did not believe our systems were so pathetic that they needed to be reinvented, but rather promoted the belief that over time, existing systems could be improved significantly.

What was radical about our initiative was the new way we asked people to "think" about their jobs and the organization. We were asking our associates to change the way they approached work. We were suggesting that they apply TQM beliefs, values, and principles throughout the workplace.

Our contention was that external and internal forces are so powerful that government must change in order to survive. As you can imagine, there was strong resistance to our change initiative. It upset top management, middle management,, and front-line associates. Many associates took the position that the department was already doing quality work and therefore saw no need to change. Some even dug in their heels and made it very clear that they were not about to accept our change initiative. They would often complain that Total Quality Management was a fad, did not work, and even though it may have worked in some businesses, it wouldn't work in government.

Since fewer than 50 management positions in a department of 7,000 were political appointments and the rest were "protected" in career service, most associates were determined to live through the ordeal and take the attitude of "this too shall pass." We also found that political appointees as a whole, even though they supposedly "bought into" the governor's commitment to implement Total Quality Management in government, were no more receptive than career service personnel. We understood from the outset we could not force change, but rather would have to "inspire" it. From the beginning, our goal was to encourage associates to recognize the need for change and to accept Total Quality Management beliefs, values, and principles; however, a few years into the program, we implemented some policies that forced change. Today, we are not sure we were totally successful, for resistance and resentment, particularly by managers, is still a pervasive influence in the department.

The purpose of this chapter is to describe the key elements and critical factors that transformational leaders employ to inspire change in government. This discussion is designed for government leaders who feel the urgent need to change the way government conducts business and who are willing to devote energy to inspire others to change as well. Inspiring change is not a step-by-step process. One step to initiating change does not necessarily mean another logical step follows. Therefore, we have selected topics for discussion that we believe are the key elements and factors that, when instituted, can inspire change in organizations.

VISION

It is not uncommon for transformational leaders to assess the present state of their organization and feel the need for change. The question that is always before them is, "what should the organization become?" A leader who has answered this question has a mental image of what is possible for the organization in the future. Administrators generally have a perception of what they do not want to occur. Transformational leaders, on the other hand, have a perception of a desirable future. They not only see the organization as it is in its present state, but also have an ideal image of what the organization can become.

Inspiring others to change requires a leader to clearly understand the desired end state of the organization. It requires a vision, a mental image of the future state of the organization. For example, in Florida's Department of Labor and Employment Security, we envisioned an organization that focused on customers, organized around processes, and was data driven with associates working in teams to achieve organization goals. In the beginning, we diagnosed the organization as a top-down bureaucracy where individuals were assigned specific tasks, and where it was extremely difficult to tap the brain power of the organization's members. We believed that the department made far too many errors and was not satisfying the needs of its customers. We believed that it was time to shift from a "management-by-objectives" approach to one of "Total Quality Management." Our goal was to inspire change and to motivate associates to change the way they approached their work. We strongly believed that TQM was a far more effective management system to accomplish organization goals. Our vision required us to inspire associates in the department to accept and share our vision.

Although our vision focused on what we could create in a department of over 7,000 associates, vision is relative. It may be as simple as seeing what three or four people can achieve, or as complicated as envisioning a creation of a new direction by thousands of people. Once you are confident and believe that what you want to create is in the best interest of the organization, your challenge as a transformational leader is to inspire the team or organization to follow this vision.

SHARING THE VISION

Many people have the ability to create a mental image of what the organization could become. Few, however, have the self-confidence and inner strength to share their vision in a constructive way within their team or organization. Administrators often complain about the stupidity of those above them and, as a matter of fact, of the people below them. "If people would just listen to me, we could run this organization right," is frequently heard. However, very few ever step up to the challenge of advocating their vision of change. In traditional bureaucracies, it may be an acceptable excuse to say that they would be ignored. However, in empowerment systems, every associate has the opportunity to put forth better ideas. Creativity is not correlated to rank or level within an organization. What the organization can become is not reserved just for people at the top of the organization.

The purpose of sharing the vision is to create awareness or raise the consciousness regarding issues and consequences. For example, in Florida's Department of Labor and Employment Security, we shared our vision by personally conducting seminars on what the organization could become if we shifted our management systems from a "management-by-objectives" approach to one of TQM. We described what the organization could become and advocated a new way to achieve our goals. While a vast majority of the people attending our seminar rejected what we were advocating, we were able to persuade many that our vision would be to the benefit of the department.

We identified one of the issues as "quality" in the seminar and met significant resistance because most of our associates thought we were already a quality organization, interested in the welfare of our customers. They resented even a discussion of quality and were defensive. On the other hand, there were associates who were dissatisfied with the status quo and who were willing to listen to ideas that required change. We also identified the consequences of not changing. We advocated the position that if government could not achieve quality, the taxpayers and the legislators would either abolish the government service or turn it over to a private organization. For the most part, the consequences were not threatening since many of them had "heard it before," and more than a few informed us that they would retire "before the taxpayers and legislators caught up with them."

To articulate an inspiring vision, we suggest the following:

1. Describe the desirable and possible future of the organization. Present a picture of what the organization can be and what it could look like in five years.

2. Within the vision, include your mission statement, which provides the common purpose of organizational members.

3. Challenge the current assumptions and beliefs. Provide a new perspective, including a new set of assumptions and beliefs that should be instituted to achieve the vision.

4. Raise the consciousness of organizational members to a higher level and articulate the fact that "we are all in this together."

5. Create a sense of urgency—"Now is the time to change if we are going to improve and survive."

STRATEGY FOR PLANNED CHANGE

Armed with a vision, transformational leaders need to develop and implement a plan that achieves their visions. When a leader has concluded that maintaining the status quo is not in the best interest of the organization, it is time to convince organization members that the status quo will cause problems for them. To change attitudes and behaviors of associates, we suggest that transformational leaders engage in "planned change," deliberately designed to redirect the organization so it is in a better position to adapt to its environment and increase its organizational effectiveness.

One of the most useful models of organizational change was developed by Kurt Lewin.[1] Lewin suggested that there are two sets of forces acting on peoples' behaviors. One set of forces pushs for change while the other set of forces resists change in favor of the status quo. If both forces are exerting equal pressure, then the present level of behavior will continue, which Lewin referred to as a "quasi-stationary equilibrium." His approach argued that if you want to inspire change, then you should reduce the forces that maintain the status quo and increase the forces for change.

Lewin's approach to change requires three steps. First, you must unfreeze the culture by making people aware of the weakness in their current conditions. You can unfreeze a culture by persuading organizational members that the current organization culture will not achieve desirable outcomes.

Once you are able to unfreeze the organization and are able to motivate associates to look for a better way to achieve organization goals, you can proceed to the second stage in the process. Lewin refers to the second step as the "organization changing," or an organization in transition. It is during this transition that associates embrace new beliefs, values, and attitudes towards the organization and it's customers. It is during this phase that transformational leaders use various interventions to move the organization in the desired direction. New work methods, management systems, structures, strategies, and technology are introduced to help associates adapt to change.

The third and final step in Lewin's model of change is the process of refreezing, where the changes become institutionalized. For example, in Florida's Department of Labor and Employment Security, after we were able to unfreeze traditional attitudes and beliefs and implement desirable changes, we then attempted to refreeze the culture. We were able to shift from a management-by-objectives approach to one of Total Quality Management.

We should point out, however, that we do not have the same concept of "refreezing the organization" as Lewin had fifty years ago. What we mean by "refreeze" is to develop a culture that is constantly preparing for change. When transformational leaders implement Total Quality Management, they are creating a climate that is open to change. They are constantly adjusting their organization by making continual improvements. Transformational leaders are creating cultures where attitudes and behavior continually contribute to organization change. Therefore, transformational leaders are refreezing the organization to a culture that continually pursues change and improvement.

The results of a plan change effort are often mixed. Obviously, few change initiatives turn out exactly as they were planned. Porras and Hoffer[2] found, in a survey of 42 leading organization development specialists, that employees who experienced effective change interventions will do the following:

1. Communicate more openly.

2. Collaborate more effectively.

3. Take more responsibility.

4. Maintain a shared vision.

5. Solve problems more effectively.

6. Show more respect and support for others.

7. Interact with each other more effectively.

8. Be more inquisitive.

9. Be more open to experimentation and new ways of doing things.

INTERVENTIONS

Inspiring change in government requires the use of specific methods to bring about the desired change. These methods—interventions—require leaders to intervene in the ongoing system. Interventions are designed to improve organizational effectiveness. They are injected into the system to intentionally cause changes in attitudes and behaviors. Over the years numerous intervention strategies have been identified and tested. Some of the more predominant interventions have included job enlargement, job rotation, sensitivity training, assessment centers, managerial grid, quality of work life, team building, conflict resolution, survey feedback, transactional analysis, stress management, management-by-objectives, flex time, quality circles, career planning, autonomous work groups, reengineering, open book management, Total Quality Management, etc.

Some of the intervention strategies were directed towards helping individuals to change, improving interpersonal relationships, or promoting teamwork, while other interventions were employed at implementing system-wide change.

Transformational leaders use a wide variety of interventions to promote change. Since their goal is to empower the total work force, transformational leaders cause interventions that enable workers to solve problems and take responsibility for their decisions. This is a formidable challenge since empowerment is more of a concept in government than a reality. Inspiring change to an empowerment system requires the careful selection and timing of specific interventions.

For example, when we sought to empower the workforce in the Department of Labor and Employment Security, we selected the beliefs and principles of Total Quality Management. We believed that if we could inject TQM beliefs and principles into the system, it would lead to an empowered workforce. While we have been able to make some progress in empowering the work force over the years, the results of our efforts have been mixed. At this writing, we are in the fourth year of our TQM intervention, and there is still significant resistance towards empowering the workforce. Deming and Juran warned us of the time it would take to change traditional organizations to Total Quality Managed ones. They told us that TQM was not a program, but an initiative that required significant time and energy. They were right.

System-wide change in a government organization is a journey that has many obstacles. In fact, it is doubtful that, no matter what intervention is selected to empower the workforce, it will work right the first time. It took years for management-by-objectives to be ingrained into a system. We believe it is much more difficult to empower a workforce than it was to implement management-by-objectives. Furthermore, empowering the workforce will require a series of interventions directed by transformational leaders who inspire change. We suggest the use of the following intervention techniques to inspire associates to become an empowered work force.

1. Design and promote top management team-building sessions where vision, mission, and empowering principles are articulated.

2. Design and promote top management training seminars in customer focus, process orientation, quality management tools, and team development.

3. Develop and publish the vision of the organization.

4. Develop and publish the organization's mission statement.

5. Develop and publish the organization's values.

6. Develop and publish the management principles of an empowered team-based organization.

7. Train all administrators to be transformational leaders, from top management to supervisors. Convince them to accept the beliefs and principles of an empowered organization and to practice the principles of transformational leadership.

8. Train all organization members on how to focus on the customer, how to manage processes, how to use quality tools, and how to work in teams.

9. Encourage top management to be members of process improvement teams.

10. Form project teams, cross-functional teams, process improvement teams and, if you are a risk-taker, form self-managed teams.

11. Flowchart the entire organization, followed by identification of process boundaries, suppliers, and customers.

12. Survey the organization continually and use survey feedback to make adjustments in your planned change strategy.

13. Publicize the quality improvements via your internal newsletter with photos of successful teams.

14. Have a Celebration Day where the Governor, key legislators, and the press are invited to view and appreciate your success.

15. Establish a formal recognition system for honoring individuals and teams that significantly contribute to improving the organization.

OVERCOMING RESISTANCE TO CHANGE

When you try to advance a new order, you will no doubt meet significant resistance. It is natural for people to resist things that they do not understand. When they do not understand something, they become uncertain and begin to wonder how the changes advanced will affect them. The question always before them is "how do I benefit" from the change.

Later in this chapter we will address the challenge of getting people to put organizational interests above their own and the special qualities of a leader who can get them to do so. Here, we are concerned with ways to reduce resistance that occur with most change initiatives.

Dealing with change in today's work environment is a daily occurrence. A problem that leaders encounter with change is that people believe the suggested changes will not be to their benefit. When system-wide changes are proposed, anxiety and uncertainty are likely to emerge. Therefore, it is the leader's responsibility to reduce anxiety and uncertainty by showing how the proposed change will benefit associates. For example, when we instituted a system-wide change in Florida's Department of Labor and Employment Security, many people were very uncomfortable. Hundreds of reasons were expressed as to why our change initiative would be unsuccessful. Perhaps most interesting was the significant resistance we received from upper management. For years top management had complained about how front-line workers resisted change. However, when we instituted a change that they perceived was not in their best interest, managers strongly resisted. When upper management perceived that the change we were advocating was not in their best interest, they began to behave just like the people about whom they complained.

Even today, many top managers significantly resist empowering associates within their departments. The problem with government administrators is that many believe that management should be for their own convenience and not for the convenience of their subordinates or customers. Many are still enamored of their positions and want to retain position power. Overcoming their resistance is perhaps the most significant challenge to changing government. Many are very insecure and fear the loss of power and perhaps the loss of their positions. One of the problems of initiating system-wide empowerment is that administrators will lose their power to control individuals. However, they gain power in controlling processes. Therefore, to inspire change, transformational leaders have to convince administrators or else remove those who are not willing to personally accept the benefits derived from an empowerment system.

Even though front-liners initially resist empowerment systems, they are often eager to change once they understand that it not only benefits them but the organization as well. The real challenge for transformational leaders is to persuade their administrators that they too can benefit by changing from administrators to transformational leaders. Although they may lose position power, they gain control over their processes. Sometimes administrators are so resistant to change that the only way to convince them to change is to have them perceive economic losses or loss of position before they will change.

Transformational leaders in government realize that it is very difficult to remove administrators who resist system-wide change. Therefore, they must rely on their ability to influence administrators to accept the benefits of an empowered workforce, and to persuade them to adopt the principles of transformational leadership. They need to clearly understand the organization's vision and mission and assist the organization in achieving the desired culture.

ACCESSING CHANGE

Accessing the effects of interventions in an organization is always a difficult challenge. Organizations commonly review reports, examine records, survey members, review critical incidents, and conduct surveys. Honeywell Space Systems in Clearwater, Florida, monitored their change initiative by inviting employees to participate regularly in focus groups. They also regularly surveyed their managers and carefully tracked results.

The origin of any assessment tool stems directly from the organization's vision. The clearer the vision, the easier it is to develop assessment measurement tools. Since we strongly believe that empowering the workforce is the critical factor to organizational effectiveness, we developed an assessment tool that we believe measures whether an organization is positively changing towards an empowerment system. This survey can be administered system-wide in specific units to teams, or can be used to facilitate discussion in focus groups.

EMPOWERMENT SYSTEMS SURVEY

		Agree				Disagree
1.	I am encouraged to work on teams.	5	4	3	2	1
2.	I have the freedom to make changes in my process.	5	4	3	2	1
3.	We have time for team meetings.	5	4	3	2	1
4.	There is mutual respect and trust within my work team.	5	4	3	2	1
5.	I am challenged to find new problems in my processes.	5	4	3	2	1
6.	My supervisor supports our team.	5	4	3	2	1
7.	My supervisor provides recognition for team work.	5	4	3	2	1
8.	My supervisor communicates confidence in my team.	5	4	3	2	1
9.	Our team uses quality tools effectively.	5	4	3	2	1
10.	Our team has identified and knows our customers.	5	4	3	2	1
11.	We try to meet or exceed customer expectations.	5	4	3	2	1
12.	My supervisor encourages empowerment training.	5	4	3	2	1
13.	Our team meetings are enjoyable.	5	4	3	2	1
14.	Top management "walks the talk."	5	4	3	2	1
15.	I am committed to this organization.	5	4	3	2	1

Objective evaluations are effective sources for monitoring change initiatives. Other methods such as visiting teams, observing team presentations, attending recognition ceremonies, listening to stories, monitoring rumors, benchmarking processes against the best, or even being a devil's advocate are effective methods to gather information regarding the effectiveness of your change initiative.

INSTITUTIONALIZING CHANGE

As the organization is transformed to the desired state, you begin the process of institutionalizing your change initiative. The most effective method for institutionalizing change is to develop systems that reward and recognize those who perform well. Performance appraisals are rewritten. Job descriptions are rewritten. Recruitment and job selection criteria are rewritten. All reflect what you want to occur in your organization. In empowerment systems, your criteria will include the individual's ability to work cohesively within teams and to use scientific methods to improve organization processes.

Another method of institutionalizing change is to recognize and reinforce associates who exhibit desired empowerment behaviors. Thus you provide associates with what they want in exchange for successful performance. Furthermore, you use the media to celebrate their performance and achieve the recognition they justly deserve. You can also institutionalize change by encouraging learning, freely distributing information, supporting continual improvement, valuing experimentation, and by selecting people on the basis of their ability to learn rather than solely on their knowledge and formal education. Another method is to restructure the organization to reflect empowerment systems, organize around processes, flatten the organization, and reduce the number of administrators. Ultimately, to institutionalize change you need a reward system that reinforces the new way of doing things.

INSPIRATION

Transformational leaders are inspirational leaders. They motivate their followers to achieve greater heights. They challenge their followers, excite their emotions, and unite them to find new ways to improve their organization and to positively affect outcomes.

Transformational leaders inspire enthusiasm and excitement in followers. In some instances, they must inspire associates to accomplish goals that transcend their own self-interest. For example, many transformational leaders are willing to sacrifice their position power for the best interest of the organization. These leaders understand that empowerment systems will often cause them to lose position power, yet they are willing to put their personal power interest aside in the interest of serving their customers more effectively. Transformational leaders build commitment to the organization and raise associates to higher levels of performance by appealing to higher ideals. They stimulate or inspire associates not by solely relying on exchanging rewards for compliance, but rather by communicating an appealing vision and model of desirable behavior.

Associates are more likely to become inspired when they perceive the situation to be urgent and requiring immediate action. For example, many government workers have been strongly influenced by recent voter attitudes and legislator concerns. The continual criticism by the news media, taxpayers, and customers have definitely had an impact on government workers. Many realize that government must change, must focus on customers, and must reduce waste. These events frequently make government workers more receptive to leaders who can articulate a vision of change. When associates "buy in" to the new vision, the leader reinforces their perception, and inspires further change by fabricating a path that associates can follow to the desired organizational state. Furthermore, the leader works with associates to reduce roadblocks and pitfalls.

Inspiration to change stems from not merely developing a vision, but from making a commitment to the vision. If associates believe that leadership is committed to the vision, they are more likely to be committed and to trust their leaders. Commitment and trust evolve from associates perceiving leaders as having their best interest, as well as those of the organization, at heart. It is difficult to gain commitment and trust if leaders shift their positions frequently and express contradictory values. Transformational leaders cannot be inconsistent in articulating their vision and role modeling organization values.

Inspiring others requires transformational leaders to have strong convictions regarding their beliefs, values, and principles, as well as their vision. They are emotionally involved and committed. They are willing to take risks and put forth dynamic energy. Above all, they have high expectations of themselves, as well as their associates. They strongly believe in their associates and have confidence in their abilities and skills. Furthermore, they believe in an ignited and a united workforce. They are willing to make personal sacrifices, such as being the first person to arrive at work, going where associates work rather than having them come to their office, and being exposed to associate criticism and customer complaints. Finally, they are flexible, are able to tolerate uncertainty and willing to learn from their experience.

Transforming government organizations to empowerment systems requires leaders to inspire associates to shift their traditional beliefs and values to empowerment beliefs and values. To be successful, transformational leaders will have to go beyond the typical approaches to change in organization. It is doubtful that transformational leaders will be successful if they attempt to rely on issuing "decrees" or rules that dictate one way of doing things, by replacing people to improve performance, or by changing the structure of the organization. To successfully institute empowerment systems, transformational leaders will have to rely more on their personal influence, their ability to convince associates that their ideas work not only for the benefit of the organization, but also to the benefit of the associates. Not only will the organization be more effective in achieving desirable outcomes, but also the self-esteem of associates will be increased.

Transformational leaders influence associates to internalize the motives and rationale for change. In other words, associates must be convinced that when they adopt the new vision, they will be more effective in coping with external and internal tension and believe that the new system helps them to deliver effective government service. They need to believe that by adopting a new conceptual framework of how work is accomplished in the organization, they will be able to better contribute to achieving organization outcomes.

Empowering the workforce is the key to improving government efficiency and effectiveness. It is even sometimes difficult to comprehend the possibilities of what government could become if millions of people went to work every day with the intent, and even more importantly, the opportunity to collectively use their brain power to improve government operations. For this desired state to become a reality, transformational leaders must emerge in government. Inspiring government workers to achieve greater heights and to accept the responsibility for continually improving government organizations is indeed a worthy challenge. However, for those who are dependent upon government, as well as for those people dedicated to government work, the outcome will be extremely rewarding.

Endnotes

1. Kurt Lewin, *Field Theory in Social Sciences.* New York: Harper and Row, 1951.

2. J.I. Porras and S.J. Hoffer. "Common Behavior Changes in Successful Organization Development," *Journal of Applied Behavioral Science*, 22(1986), 477–494.

BIBLIOGRAPHY

Bass, B.M. *Leadership and Performance Beyond Expectations.* New York: The Free Press, 1985.

———. *Handbook of Leadership: A Survey of Theory and Research.* New York: Free Press, 1990.

Bennis, W.G. *On Becoming a Leader.* Reading, MA: Addison-Wesley, 1989.

Bennis, W.G., and B. Nanus. *Leaders: The Strategies for Taking Charge.* New York: Harper & Row, 1985.

Bettin, P.J., and J.K. Kennedy, Jr. "Leadership experience and leader performance: Some empirical support at last." *Leadership Quarterly* 1 (1990): 219–228.

Bradley, R.T. *Charisma and Social Power: A Study of Love and Power, Wholeness and Transformation.* New York: Paragon, 1987.

Bryman, A. *Charisma and Leadership in Organizations.* London: Sage, 1992.

Burns, J.M. *Leadership.* New York: Harper & Row, 1978.

Cohen, A.R., and D.L. Bradford. *Influence without Authority.* New York: Wiley, 1990.

Conger, J.A. *The Charismatic Leader.* San Francisco: Jossey-Bass, 1989.

Eisenstat, R.A., and S.G. Cohen. Summary: Top Management Groups. In *Groups That Work (and Those That Don't),* edited by J.R. Hackman, 78–88. San Francisco: Jossey-Bass, 1990.

Fiedler, F.E., and J.E. Garcia. *New Approaches to Leadership: Cognitive Resources and Organizational Performance.* New York: Wiley, 1987.

Gardner, J.W. *On Leadership.* New York: Free Press, 1990.

Hackman, J.R. *Groups That Work (and Those That Don't).* San Francisco: Jossey-Bass, (1990).

House, R.J., J. Woycke, and E.M. Fodor. Charismatic and Noncharismatic Leaders: Differences in Behavior and Effectiveness. In *Charismatic Leadership: The Elusive Factor in Organizational Effectiveness,* edited by J.A. Conger and R.N. Kanungo, 81–98. San Francisco: Jossey-Bass, 1988.

Hunt, J.G. *Leadership: A New Synthesis.* Newbury Park, CA: Sage, 1991.

Jermier, J.M., and L.J. Berkes. "Leader behavior in a police command bureaucracy: A closer look at the quasi-military model." *Administrative Science Quarterly* 24 (1979): 1–23.

Juran, J.M. *Juran on Leadership for Quality.* New York: Free Press, 1989.

Kanter, R.M. *The Change Master.* New York: Simon & Schuster, 1983.

Kerr, S., and J.M. Jermier. "Substitutes for leadership: Their meaning and measurement." *Organizational Behavior and Human Performance* 22 (1978): 375–403.

Kotter, J.P. *The Leadership Factor.* New York: Free Press, 1988.

———. "Power and influence: Beyond final authority." *Macmillan Executive Summary Program* (September 1985): 1–8.

Kouzes, J.M., and B.Z. Posner. *The Leadership Challenge: How to Get Extraordinary Things Done in Organizations.* San Francisco: Jossey-Bass, 1987.

Lippitt, R. "The changing leader-follower relationships of the 1980s." *Journal of Applied Behavioral Science* 18 (1982): 395–403.

Lord, R.G., and K.J. Maher. *Leadership and Information Processing: Linking Perceptions and Performance.* Boston: Unwin-Hyman, 1991.

Marcus, J.T. "Transcendence and charisma." *The Western Political Quarterly* 16 (1961): 236–41.

McClelland, D.C. *Power: The Inner Experience.* New York: Irvington (distributed by Halstead Press), 1975.

McGregor, D. *Leadership and Motivation.* Cambridge, MA: MIT Press, 1966.

Mowday, R.T. "Leader characteristics, self-confidence, and methods of upward Influence in organizational decision situations." *Academy of Management Journal* 22 (1979): 709–25.

Peters, T.J., and N. Austin. A *Passion for Excellence: The Leadership Difference.* New York: Random House, 1985.

Sashkin, M.A. "A new vision of leadership." *Journal of Management Development* 6 (1987): 19–28.

Sashkin, M.A. The Visionary Leader. In *Charismatic Leadership: The Elusive Factor in Organizational Effectiveness,* edited by J.A. Conger and R.N. Kanungo. San Francisco: Jossey-Bass, 1988.

Schein, E.H. *Organizational Culture and Leadership: A Dynamic View.* San Francisco: Jossey-Bass, 1985.

Schmidt, W.H., and B.Z. Posner. "Values and expectations of federal service executives." *Public Administration Review* 46 (1986): 447–54.

Seltzer, J., and B.M. Bass. "Transformational leadership: Beyond initiation and consideration." *Journal of Management* 16 (1990): 693–703.

Semler, R. "Managing without managers." *Harvard Business Review* (September-October, 1989): 76–84.

Shamir, B., R.J. House, and M.B. Arthur. "The motivational effects of charismatic leadership: A self-concept based theory." *Organization Science* 4 (1993): 1–17.

Sims, H.P., and A.D. Szilagyi. "Leader reward behavior and subordinate satisfaction and performance." *Organizational Behavior and Human Performance* 14 (1975): 426–38.

Tichy, N.M., and M.A. Devanna. *The Transformational Leader.* New York: Wiley, 1986.

Trice, H.M., and J.M. Beyer. *The Cultures of Work Organizations.* Engelwood Cliffs, NJ: Prentice Hall, 1993.

———. Charisma and Its Routinization in Two Social Movement Organizations. In *Research in Organizational Behavior*, Vol. 8, edited by B.M. Staw and L.L. Cummings. Greenwich, CT: JAI, 1986.

Tucker, R.C. "The theory of charismatic leadership." *Daedalus* 97 (1968): 731–56.

Waldman, D.A., B.M. Bass, and F.J. Yammarino. "Adding to contingent reward behavior: The augmenting effect of charismatic leadership." *Group and Organization Studies* 15 (1990): 381–91.

Weflins, R.S., W.C. Byham, and J.M. Wilson. *Empowered Teams: Creating Self-Directed Work groups That Improve Quality, Productivity, and Participation.* San Francisco: Jossey-Bass, 1991.

Willner, A.R. *The Spellbinders: Charismatic Political Leadership.* New Haven, CT: Yale University Press, 1984.

Yukl, G.A. *Leadership in Organizations.* 3rd ed. Englewood Cliffs, NJ: Prentice Hall, 1994.

Yukl, G., and B. Tracey. "Consequences of influence tactics used with subordinates, peers, and the boss." *Journal of Applied Psychology* 77 (1992): 525–35.

INDEX